Once Upon a Murder

Once Upon a Murder

Andrew Keogh Ruotolo, M.D.

GROSSET & DUNLAP
A FILMWAYS COMPANY
Publishers • New York

The author and publisher gratefully acknowledge permission to include material from the following:

"The Love Song of J. Alfred Prufrock" in *Collected Poems 1909-1963* by T. S. Eliot. Copyright © 1936 by Harcourt Brace Jovanovich, Inc.; copyright © 1963, 1964 by T. S. Eliot. Reprinted by permission of Harcourt Brace Jovanovich, Inc.

Courtroom: The Story of Samuel S. Leibowitz by Quentin Reynolds. Copyright © 1950 by Quentin Reynolds. Copyright renewed 1978 by James J. Reynolds. Reprinted by permission of Farrar, Straus & Giroux, Inc.

To Kill a Mockingbird by Harper Lee. Copyright © 1960 by Harper Lee. Reprinted by permission of J. B. Lippincott Company.

The Poems of Emily Dickinson edited by Thomas H. Johnson, Cambridge, Mass.: The Belknap Press of Harvard University Press. Copyright © 1951, 1955 by the President and Fellows of Harvard College. Reprinted by permission of the publishers and trustees of Amherst College.

Peter Pan by James Barrie. Copyright © 1911 by Charles Scribner's Sons. Reprinted by permission of Charles Scribner's Sons.

Neurosis and Human Growth by Karen Horney, M.D. Copyright © 1950 by Karen Horney, M.D. Reprinted by permission of W. W. Norton & Company, Inc.

Four of the cases were described previously in the *American Journal of Psychoanalysis*.

Published simultaneously in Canada
Library of Congress catalog card number: 78-055619
First printing
ISBN 0-448-14652-5 (hardcover edition)
Printed in the United States of America

To my children—who have outgrown fairy tales

Contents

Preface

He who hates vices hates mankind.
—Thrasea
I am a man; nothing human is alien to me.
—Terence

This is a book about seven murderers or near murderers and one murderess. Although not all committed murder in the precise, legal sense of the term, each contributed or almost contributed to the unjustified death of another human being. Each one was psychiatrically examined and his or her mental condition reported to a court. The length of examinations varied between nine and fifteen hours and was frequently supplemented by the study of voluminous past psychiatric records.

As these individuals related their life stories, their inner fantasies, and the specific circumstances of their crimes, a faint leitmotiv gradually became insistent with each additional case. There seemed to be a slight focusing of each person's attention off the mark, a subtle zigging while I was zagging, a tangential interest in what I presumed to be of paramount importance under the circumstances. Each seemed to be listening to a "different drummer," and in each case, *murder seemed incidental.*

In psychoanalysis it is often said that the truth lies in a mistake. The mistake in these cases seemed to lie in my own frame of reference, in my preconception that the taking of another's life would be of transcendent importance to the murderer. As the seemingly incidental natures of the murders kept reappearing, I tried to correct for this "mistake." Instead of continuing to ignore certain nuances of their stories by inadvertently anticipating, I attempted to follow patiently, expectantly, and nonjudgmentally wherever the murderers *had* to lead me. Unconsciously they guided me deep into the labyrinths of their own minds. There, in the center, in the sanctum sanctorum, reposed the core values, the essential neurotic pride system. This neurotic pride system, with its inevitable component of enormous self-hate, was the "critical mass," the explosive mixture. When penetrated too rapidly by circumstances, in each individual a lethal explosion occurred.

The neurotic pride system in each individual was encompassed within the development of an idealized self-image. The idealized image, in turn, had developed into a unique, unifying, inner mental construct which bound a neurotically afflicted individual into a semblance of integration. It was a jerry-rigged structure, however, and prone to destruction or decompensation under certain circumstances. The case histories in this book illuminate these progressions with all their tragic consequences.

Depending on the reader's prior knowledge, interest, or perseverance regarding psychodynamic formulations, it is recommended that an out-of-sequence perusal of the Appendix might be helpful. It constitutes a thumbnail sketch of Karen Horney's theories of personality development. My own psychoanalytic training and orientation rest on her ideas, and insights into these individuals seemed especially fruitful within this frame of reference. In accordance with Horney's thinking, I have used the term *neurotic* when referring to defenses and conflicts in psychotic as well as neurotic individuals, inasmuch as she emphasized the similarities of these pathological devices in both classifications. In no way is this to imply that she did not recognize valid diagnostic distinctions between the two groups.

Acknowledgments

Many individuals contribute their labor, interest, and advice to the creation of any book. I deeply appreciate the loyal and accurate typing and correcting of several drafts by Joan B. Pennick, Ruth Stengel, and Eleanor Quackenbos. I was fortunate to be associated with dedicated and highly competent attorneys such as Stephen Maskaleris, John Stamler, Hyman Isaac, Jacob Mantel, Ernest Biro, Peter Perretti, and Judge E. Cuddie Davidson, Jr. Without their tutelage and guidance through the legal underbrush, I would never have persisted in my medico-legal endeavors. Colleagues from the American Institute for Psychoanalysis such as Drs. Theodore Isaac Rubin, Helen DeRosis, Herbert Perr, Robert Ranucci, and Douglas Ingram contributed encouragement and accurate advice at many stages of the book's development. My personal mentor throughout my psychiatric career, Dr. Donald Van Gordon, supported me from the wings and contributed ideas and flair. Esteemed teachers such as Dr. Alexander Reid Martin and Dean Harry Gershman of the American Institute for Psychoanalysis inspired me with their wisdom and inner spirit. Particular mention has to be made of Associate Dean Isidore Portnoy, who not only has been a constant model but offered constructive and precise criticism of the manuscript. Colleagues at the Seton Hall University Guidance Center such as Drs. Barbara Barrett and Joseph Spiegel also offered meaningful suggestions that have been incorporated. My family was invaluable in its enthusiasm and affection through the lows as well as the highs of every writer's travail.

Having Robert Markel as editor-in-chief and Diana Price as editor was a rare stroke of good fortune. They improved the work and inspired me by their knowledge and enthusiasm.

The drawings by Alice Brickner capture the essence of these individuals and I am grateful to her for adding this dimension to the stories. I would also like to thank Larry Gadd for the design and artistic direction of the book.

Finally this book is anchored in the theories—and perhaps even more in the spirit—of Karen Horney. There is little or nothing new regarding psychodynamic formulations that is not alluded to or encompassed by her writings. I have attempted to follow her principles of open-minded inquiry, unfailing curiosity about the diversity of human nature, and nonjudgmental respect for the innate constructive strivings, even if often thwarted, in most individuals. If the mark has been hit on occasion, much is owed to her; if mistakes in application have been made, the responsibility is mine.

Author's Note

Each individual described in this book is a real person—not a composite. However, in order to protect the protagonists and their families from needless recall of tragic memories, certain inessential facts have been altered to protect their identities. Society has exacted retribution enough for their crimes. Similarly, extended follow-ups on these individuals are not provided. In some instances such information was not available. In others it could have been obtained but was deliberately avoided. One's natural curiosity has to be restrained when it clashes with the rights to privacy of an individual. Such innate rights of the accused are temporarily suspended during legal proceedings. After the verdict has been reached and sentence imposed, the veil should be allowed to fall once again.

All the events described here actually took place, over a period of some twenty years, and almost all have been revealed in open court. Some literary license has been taken, but no contrived dénouements or ironies have been introduced. No such embellishments are necessary in most real-life murders; reality provides sufficient surprises and paradoxes.

Introduction

*And what doth the Lord require of thee, but to do
justly, and to love mercy, and to walk humbly with your God?*
—Micah 6:8

HE FIRST CRIME WAS EATING THE FRUIT OF THE TREE of knowledge. The second was Cain's slaying of Abel. This is a book about murder, the second biblical crime. Yet these true stories revolve about the first crime also; not just disobedience to God but the real crime underlying the defiance of the divine injunction—competition with Him. As Genesis states, "For God doth know that in the day ye eat thereof, then your eyes shall be opened, and *ye shall be as gods, knowing good and evil.* . . . And the Lord God said, Behold, the man is become *as one of us*, to know good and evil."

On one level every murderer acts like a god when he deprives another human being of that most priceless and irreplaceable of gifts—life. On a deeper, unconscious level these murderers played a different god-game, in their *private*

3

images of themselves. This was evident in the manner in which they formulated their values and directed their exigent yearnings. Their self-images were invested with enormously powerful emotional forces, the inevitable consequences of which were beyond their understanding. Undeniably they victimized others in this ultimate act. But they themselves were victimized also, by *thinking* they knew themselves when they knew not who they were and therefore could not truly know what they did.

As their stories unfold, you will be invited into their secret images of themselves. I have perceived them in terms of fairy-tale or legendary or even biblical characters. Some recognized and even glorified in this identification; others had no conscious awareness of any connection. But all *idealized* themselves in some grandiose fashion. Idealization as a concept may seem relatively harmless; these tales demonstrate otherwise.

Idealizing yourself means creating a secret image compounded of qualities and attributes you think you have, wish you have, assume you have, or insist you have in quantities or combinations other than you actually have. It implies a process of *arrogating* to yourself that which you don't have, and perhaps no human being has or should have in pure form. Perfection is reserved for God; to compete with Him is the height of arrogance.

"To walk humbly with your God" is not only a magnificent religious concept but a profoundly rich psychological truth. Psychologically it means to walk humbly with your God-like exaggerations of yourself—everyone has such exaggerations to some degree—to be serious about what you do without taking yourself too seriously, and finally to reach that state of genuine humility where you *know* in every fiber of your being that it is better to be real than regal. Without humility you cannot "do justly" nor "love mercy." You cannot be authentic but can merely present a facade. Values that seemed solid and sustaining will desert you, and their opposites rise suddenly and overwhelm you. Such happened with the individuals described in this book.

To idealize oneself is to construct a skyscraper resting on one brick; it looks ever so tall and ever so impressive, but its very nature predisposes it to catastrophic collapse in a strong wind. That wind was ultimately provided by a storm welling up from within the unknown regions of these individuals' emotions. Emotions that they denied in their single-minded development of God-like personality traits suddenly erupted and swept away all control in homicidal furies. They had attempted almost as fiats of the will to raise certain attributes to dizzy heights while imperiously consigning any opposing or conflicting feelings into their nether regions. But feelings are not so conveniently disposed of—they are not sleeping dogs to be let lie. They ferment in one's subterranean depths, they boil and bubble and build up pressure and finally explode, sometimes disastrously.

Self-idealization is the fundamental neurotic or psychotic way of life. It is an attempt at *smoothing out* one's inner conflicting emotions, at presenting a round, no-sharp-edges facade. To accomplish this, one has to play fast and loose to a greater or lesser extent with reality. The opposite way, "the road . . . less traveled by," is one's true road, the road meant for you and you alone. It is the search for self-realization, for authenticity of feelings, values, and goals. Robert Browning understood it when he said, "When the struggle begins within a man, then he's worth something." Alexander Reid Martin understood it when he said, "Insight comes with the awareness of one's *total* involvement in conflict." To avoid conflict, to refuse to live with one's inner hyphens is to trade ultimate, healthy satisfactions for expediency and a spurious unity.

Such false unities will be apparent in these individuals. They chose to become Johnny-one-notes, to avoid the hazards of change, to hide behind walls of familiar maneuvers and anxiety-alleviating devices. Of course they did not consciously and deliberately choose so; their early life experiences produced such anxiety due to emotional conflicts that they were overwhelmed and sought safety in fixed, often childish psychic positions rather than daring the hazards of future change and growth. But as Whitehead has said, "It is the *business* of the future to be dangerous." One has to develop a broad base, to maintain a proper sense of proportion, to be able to touch most of the strong feelings within, to remain open and tentative in the face of uncertainty, to lower one's center of gravity within one's real self—in short, "to walk humbly with your God". This allows one to bend and not break in the strong winds with which life buffets us all sooner or later.

These murderers were not able to "put away childish things" in time to prevent murder. Reality intruded in their fairy-tale idealizations of themselves and unexpectedly cut the solid ground out from under them shortly after many had made new and hazardous moves to healthier psychic positions. With no familiar psychic place on which to stand at a given moment in time and space, they lurched back to former positions of safety at the cost of forfeiting the life of another.

Fairy tales usually have happy endings; these real-life fairy tales proved to be tragically grim.

Robin Hood

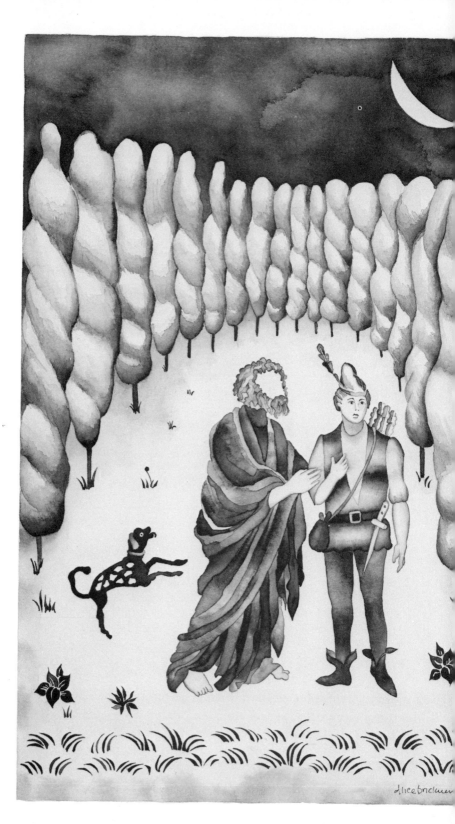

Y FIRST MEMORY, DOC, WAS OF A BANK. I MUST HAVE been five or six. I had gone with my Papa to withdraw all our money. Papa had been a hard worker all his life and saved every penny he could. We had gone without for years in order to buy a house. One crummy tenement after another . . . saving, that's all we did. At last the big day had arrived. A house of our own with grass and trees and a backyard and everything. Then this big snob refused to give Papa the money. He looked down his nose at us and droned on about runs on banks, stock-market crashes, worldwide depression, et cetera, et cetera. Neither of us knew what he was talking about. Papa kept repeating that his money *had* to be there. He had put all his savings in that solid-looking building to protect it from robbers and Cossacks. He had never given them permission to invest in the stocks or bonds or whatever. Finally, the bank official threatened to call his private policeman over and throw us out if we continued making a racket. He told my Papa to sell apples on the street corners like everyone else.

"Outside Papa said it was just like the old country after all. He had hoped America would be different. They had said here a man could work hard, save his money, and finally buy his own house. Those were the rules. But now they had changed the rules again. They had robbed him of his life. It was 1930 and the only rule was the same as in Poland, 'Money talks, a beggar walks.' We walked home without a word between us.

"I don't remember Papa talking much ever again. He just seemed to shrivel up more day by day. Shortly afterwards, he complained of this pain in the chest and couldn't breathe right. Some men came and tried to electrocute him. They connected these wires from his chest and leg to the electric socket and turned on the current. Their faces looked evil as they watched a lot of dials in this black box. The black box buzzed with electricity. They said it was only an electrocard... something, but I knew better. It was just like Jimmy Cagney getting it in the electric chair in the movies. I screamed and kicked one of the men in the shins, but he held me down. Mama was crying helplessly in the corner. When Papa wouldn't die, they strapped him to a stretcher and carried him out to their big white ambulance. They said they were taking him to a hospital. I knew they were taking him some place to finish him off where we couldn't see it. Mama told me he died that same day.

"That was the beginning of a series of mysterious deaths. Next was my dog. I came home from school one day to see another white ambulance speed away from the apartment house. Mama said my dog had died, but I knew somebody poisoned him.

"Next came Casey, the school-crossing guard. He had always been nice to me, especially after they killed Papa. Suddenly one day he was gone. They said he had been retired or expired. I looked the words up and one of them meant 'dead.' So they had killed him, too. I never saw him again.

"Finally, they took Mama away. A man who claimed to be a doctor—all I know is he was all dressed in white—said he was going to cut up my Mama. He wore a white mask. Why would an honest man be afraid to show his face? I almost fainted in that damn white corridor but instead I flew into a rage and tried to hit him. Some neighbors who had taken me to the hospital held me back. I remember screaming and crying till I fell asleep. When I woke up, they told me Mama was dead.

"At the funeral I felt completely alone for the first time in my life. People and events were a blur. The only thing I can recall was the old man coming over to me and saying everything was going to be all right. He was dressed in black like most of the others. He said he'd keep in touch with me. He said he was an old friend of my Mama, and that she was a good woman and I a good son.

"I was taken in by the people downstairs. They tried to be nice, but by then I had wised up. Everyone who was the slightest bit nice to me got it in the end. So I was nasty to them at every opportunity. They didn't realize I was doing it for their own good. I joined 'them' in masking my feelings. It was the only way, the only safe way.

"As I grew older, I discovered that some nuns who taught me hated me, too. I told off those I liked to protect them from harm and was nice to those I didn't like. Gradually things became somewhat confusing. I'd lose track of which group was which and didn't know when to be nice. I finally kept my distance from all grown-ups. It was much simpler that way.

"I started playing hooky and hanging out with older guys. They let me run with the pack, but I fancied myself a lone wolf. I was with them but not of them. I used to read a lot and go to movies; gangster and adventure ones mostly. My heroes were Edward G. Robinson, Jimmy Cagney, and later Humphrey Bogart. They were neat the way they sneered at the world but were true to themselves and their pals. Mostly I liked Robin Hood. He had his own forest to retreat to, with trees and grass and animals. Everybody and everything in the forest was free. It was dark and shady there, and Robin Hood could be safe. He had his own merry band. He even had his own priest, Friar Tuck, so he couldn't have been doing much wrong. I remember making up phrases like 'I sure would like to be in Sherwood in the evening,' which I sang to the tune of 'Carolina in the Morning.'

"Then I started getting in trouble with the law. The older guys would knock over a store and then run like hell. I was the smallest so I'd get caught as I couldn't run as fast. Finally, a judge sent me away. I was lonely in that reformatory without my pals. The old man—you know, the one at Mama's funeral—visited me there. He said he'd meet me when I got out and show me this dog he had. He promised to visit me again, and he kept his word. His visits always cheered me up, as I'd be feeling especially low, it seems, at those times.

"After I was back on the streets, I took a room in a boardinghouse. I started working at odd jobs. After a few months on a job, some of the other guys would start making nasty cracks. They called me a dumb Polack and were jealous of my reading books all the time. I used to like to read and learn big words. But I never tried to impress anyone with my new words. I remembered Papa's phrase, 'Money talks, a beggar walks,' so I kept to myself pretty much. Usually I'd get fed up with the job and quit and look for another one. I never could seem to hold onto any money.

"What with one thing and another, my poor work record, no education, and reformatory background, jobs started getting scarcer. I took to wandering around alone at night. That's when I started running into the old man more often. He showed me his dog, a black-and-white spotted mutt, and I patted it for hours, it seemed. I told him how I used to look in people's windows at night because the lights made it seem warm and friendly inside. Occasionally, I'd see money or valuables just lying around, and I'd crawl through a window and take things. The old man didn't see anything wrong in that as long as the houses were big and owned by rich people. We both seemed to like to walk about at night and just talk. It was about this time I started realizing I disliked the daylight more and more. All that goddamn whiteness and glare. I felt much safer at night. People left you alone more after dark.

"I became less and less nervous about entering people's houses. Once I had their money, they would be quiet. Then I'd go to a special bar. Strange and wondrous things would happen there. I'd start drinking some and set up drinks for people I'd meet there; and I could talk to them. I'd talk and talk. They talked back, and some even said they thought I was funny. I was good at impersonations, especially of my favorite screen tough guys. When I hid behind someone else's personality, I was fluent, witty, and . . . and . . . more at ease. These were my true friends, the night people. Some were musicians, cocktail waitresses, even hookers. Some had no known means of livelihood like me. I didn't pry into their affairs, and they didn't pry into mine. As long as I was setting up drinks they'd listen. I was like an old nickelodeon; when the money ran out, my song ran down. Then I'd get morose and silent. My friends respected that and would leave me alone.

"Once I pulled a job in Brooklyn, got caught, and was hauled up in front of a judge. He was a short, balding sort of man, but he looked tough. His name was Sam Leibowitz, somebody said. I was just a kid and nervous, but I sure wasn't going to let him know it. Just as he was about to pass sentence, I gave him my best 'what the hell' look and lit up a fag. The judge flew into a rage and told me to get rid of the cigarette that instant. I tried to cover up by flipping the fag into a basket but misfired. It landed right on the good judge's robes. That really set him off. He called me a hardened hood and a potential murderer and threatened to 'throw away the key.' He called me the 'baby-faced bandit,' and the name stuck. I made the front page of the *New York Daily News* and five years in the state pen. Even created a brief stir up in stir (ha!) when I arrived complete with my newspaper clippings.

"Finally, I got out of there. I decided I'd try to break my old habits. I joined the merchant marine. They were the best years of my life. As long as I did my job and minded my own business, they left me alone. I had a lot of time to read and walk the deck at night. Nobody hassled me. I used to love to stand at the bow in the dark and feel the wind rush by. I was moving while standing still. Most of my runs were to South America. We put in up and down the east coast ports. I particularly liked Brazil. Once I had several weeks off there and took a trip into the forests—they call them rain forests. I liked the Mato Grosso best of all. When I'd return to the port I'd be struck even more by the widespread poverty and filth. It was appalling. The kids were the worst off of all. They looked so hungry and bewildered. Because I bought candy and pop for some, I'd have a mob around me in no time flat. Once I took a group of kids to a shoe store and made them all buy shoes. I paid. They thought that was queer but went along with it. 'Money talks, a beggar walks,' perhaps, but not barefoot.

"I had to leave the ships during a recession. I had no trade and no money. A guy I knew sold me a gun. It was all silver and shiny. I took really good care of it. Even scratched my initials on the barrel. I ran into the old man again. I told him about some of my travels and how I had met many people much poorer than I. It occurred to both of us at almost the same time that some of the apartments I had been burglarizing might belong to poor people. It wasn't right to take money from them, only from the rich. The solution was obvious; since banks were rich, concentrate on them. I remembered the nuns told us our Lord overthrew the tables of the money changers. And didn't Robin Hood rob only the nobles and that rich Sheriff of Nottingham? My path was clear.

"After a few successes, my luck ran out. I entered a savings and loan association, pulled my gun, and told everyone to keep quiet and give me all the money. I had it all in a sack and was ready to leave when this bank official came out of an office and yelled something at me. I was so surprised that anyone could talk, let alone yell, when I had all the money, that I whirled and pulled the trigger. Nothing happened. I pulled the trigger again. Still nothing. I panicked and ran. I was so disorganized I couldn't think straight and was captured easily by the police.

"As the police were driving me to the station, I kept telling them some of the money was mine. They showed me the bank wrappers and laughed at me. They didn't seem to understand what I was trying to tell them.

"So that's the story, Doc. I've been here in jail awaiting trial ever since. You're the fourth shrink I've seen. There's nothing wrong with my head, the other three said so to my face.

"The old man with the dog? Yes, I've seen him recently. He visits me regularly. Can't bring the dog in, of course. Why do you ask? The other shrinks didn't. He's just my special friend. Who is he? I don't know, as I never asked him, and he never volunteered. What does his voice sound like? It's deep and sounds like it comes from a cavern, like from a distance. What does he look like? He's tall and sort of old and always dresses in black. What does his face look like? *He doesn't have a face; he doesn't need one.* Is there anything else special about him? Well, now that you mention it, though I never knew this in the beginning, lately I've realized he can do lots of things. He used to visit me only during visiting hours. Now he comes right into my cell at night, and we talk as long as we want. Then he just disappears. He recently told me he can foretell the future. He can also fly. [No beggarly walking for him.] He finally told me that all the riches of the world are rightfully his. Because I am his best and truest friend, if I help him he will eventually give them all to me. After that, we're going to fly together to a mountain peak in the Mato Grosso. I know the spot well. We're going to stand together on this peak, and all the people in the world will eventually file in a silent procession below us. He'll teach me how to tell the rich-bad from the poor-good. When I finally can distinguish between them without making any errors, the old man is going to disappear for the last time. I'll order all the rich-bad into a sunny desert on my left, and all the poor-good into a shady forest on my right, and the good people will be happy there, and gaze up at me and love me forever."

And So to Court

The legal machinery moved swiftly at first. Robin was declared psychotic in a sanity hearing and remanded to a hospital for the criminally insane. The staff at the hospital declared him "apparently cured" six months after admission. Such a speedy resolution of a massive, fixed, paranoid system of delusional thinking of sixteen years' standing would be comparable to curing an inoperable case of cancer by judicious administration of aspirin. There is a simpler explanation: The withdrawn Robin merely ceased mentioning his grand design, and no staff member was so inconsiderate as to bring up the embarrassing subject. So another medical miracle sprang forth to bloom within an institutional garden.

Upon Robin's discharge from the hospital, some unidentified official returned him to a penitentiary in another state. By plucking a phrase here and half a phrase there, this benighted bureaucrat determined from the court record that Robin had violated the conditions of his parole from that state by willfully and perniciously consorting with individuals of known criminal tendencies: the old man with the dog. (At least it is reassuring to note that steps were not taken to have the spotted dog destroyed as a menace to society.) Thus, in an O. Henry twist, the very delusional proof of Robin's psychiatric psychosis was used as evidence of his legal culpability. Such are the ways of bureaucracy, unfortunately.

One year after Robin's trial, a new attorney contacted me by phone. Robin, being now completely cured in the eyes of the law, had been assigned to work in the prison library. Putting his considerable intellectual talents to work, he had delved into some legal tomes and drawn up a precise and valid writ of habeas corpus. He intended to sue the savings and loan association for his rightful portion of the $18,500 in his possession at the time of his arrest. The attorney was puzzled by the fact that Robin was claiming precisely $6,750 of the $18,500 stolen. Robin remained steadfast and adamant in the matter and was attempting to force the savings and loan association to show cause why that sum was not his.

Suddenly, it occurred to me that this was the exact amount of Robin's father's savings lost in the bank closure. I so informed the attorney. Since to a schizophrenic's primitive reasoning, similarities are identities, Robin's father's bank and the savings and loan association Robin had robbed were one and the same. (In fact, the savings and loan association had not even been in existence during the Depression.) Consequently, Robin felt he was simply reclaiming his rightful inheritance. I expressed my admiration for Robin's innate noblesse oblige which prevented him from demanding as well the considerable interest on his inheritance which would have accumulated over the years. No grubbing money changer he! All Robin expected was simple justice. He remained so calm and reasonable throughout the preliminary jousting that prison officials were completely nonplused. Some even began to doubt their own position. The complexities and inevitable expenses of the prospective proceedings involving a hearing on the writ of habeas corpus, a civil suit against the savings and loan association, possible extradition, and another superfluous sanity hearing staggered the imagination and produced a sharp pain in my taxpayer's pocketbook. Since Robin was indigent, all these prospective legal proceedings would have to be underwritten by the state. From this expensive little comedy of errors I firmly excused myself. The suits and countersuits clogged the court calendars of two states for several years.

The Illness

It was not until the correct lever was fortuitously pushed that the true extent of Robin's psychopathology was laid bare. When his delusional system of thinking, which pivoted on the identity of his imaginary and hallucinated construct, the old man with the dog, was finally revealed, it was apparent he was suffering from a chronic schizophrenic illness of the paranoid type. To disabuse the reader of any doubts about the authenticity of this delusional system, it should be borne in mind that three psychiatrists had missed the significance of his mysterious friend. Robin was not a malingerer. One does not conceal from three interviewers and finally reveal to a fourth (and then only on the third interview) if one is consciously lying; the risks are too great to a sane mind. Robin, like so many schizophrenics, was preoccupied with his inner fantasy life for his own purposes, rather than escaping a prison sentence. Besides, he sincerely perceived nothing abnormal about his thinking. He just saw himself as fortunate to have been selected as special among all others to be befriended by this rather remarkable personage. As Robin Hood eventually was contacted by a mysterious, hooded figure who turned out to be the ransomed King Richard the Lion-Hearted, so was Robin contacted by his deus ex machina. As Robin Hood joined forces with King Richard to regain the latter's rightful kingdom from the evil usurper, King John, so did our Robin plan on assisting his benefactor in regaining what was rightfully his. Only Robin took the legend one step further: to regain the entire world.

One of the classic symptoms of schizophrenia manifested by Robin was diurnal reversal—turning day into night. Because of their chronic, incapacitating anxiety and discomfort with human contact, some schizophrenics prefer the night, when they can wander about without interference. Robin also made many associations of white and daylight with danger, and black and nighttime with safety: The physicians whom he believed killed both his parents and his dog were dressed in white, whereas the old man was invariably dressed in black. Perhaps the white and black spotted dog symbolized an unconsciously felicitous rapprochement. So, too, the "good-poor" people's valley was shady and dark; the sun-drenched desert was reserved for the "bad-rich."

The remarkable feature of Robin's grand design, his messianic mission to redress the iniquities of the world, was that it was sixteen years aborning. Slowly, insidiously, and with loving care, it had been unconsciously developed, modified, expanded, and embellished. It was his creative masterpiece, his raison d'être, his magnificent delusion. It was patiently nurtured from its simple beginnings as a charity for barefoot Brazilian children until it had grown to encompass the entire world in its cosmic benevolence. This is the typical pathogenesis or natural course of such delusions; they become more and more extensive until their grandiosity assumes the proportion of a closed-system Weltanschauung. One can even trace how it had sprung from the primary defect of the preschizophrenic: the inability to abstract. This underlying defect, this concretization of thought processes, accounts for the young Robin's literal interpretation of the proverb, "Money talks, a beggar walks." In accordance with his understanding of this axiom, Robin laid the cornerstone for the elaborate superstructure of interlocking delusions and hallucinations he constructed over the next two decades.

Robin's particular secrecy and joy in exclusive possession contributed to the errors in evaluation by several penal psychologists and psychiatrists. It is ironic that in psychiatry more than in any other medical specialty, the more extensive and severe the pathology, the more difficult it often is to ferret out. The newly sick are often blatantly disturbed and confused, attempting, albeit pathologically, to evolve a new equilibrium, a modus operandi, with a world they never made. The chronically ill, on the other hand, have finally succeeded in reshaping the world of reality into one more to their liking, where they establish new and more satisfactory ground rules. Of necessity they have to break with reality to accomplish this. Consequently, they often appear relatively well adjusted to the casual observer unless he probes to the heart of their underlying premises. Usually the patient hinders rather than assists the examiner by laying down a denser smoke screen of vagueness and ambiguity, the nearer the cherished delusions are approached. This marked vagueness, in regard to the old man, for example, when superimposed on Robin's characteristically wispy and impersonal identification of the other individuals who tangentially touched his life, obfuscated the psychiatrists' vision considerably.

The second fundamental defect specifically diagnostic of schizophrenia was Robin's taking recourse in psychological causality from an early age. His father underwent a harmless electrocardiogram and subsequently died of heart disease; his mother expired from postoperative complications; and a friendly policeman was routinely retired; yet Robin attributed all his misfortunes to the deliberate malevolence of others: "They hated me!" Physical causality, the inevitable vicissitudes of reality, was unacceptable; thus the recourse to a more primitive mode of thinking, namely, psychological causality. He operated on the more primitive level of thinking typical of the magical, superstitious belief in demonology of savage tribes and our own ancient forebears. To Robin, people, not accidents of nature, accounted for *all* the world's unhappiness. Such malevolent persons, perforce, assume almost supernatural powers to a schizophrenic like Robin. What more logical solution to such a terrifying situation would appear to a lonely, frightened boy than to bind himself with hoops of steel to the most omniscient and omnipotent personage he could construct?

And so the old man, his alter ego, came into being. To counteract the private police force "they" employed, Robin now possessed his very own genie to assist him in bringing to ultimate fruition his grand design. The more he withdrew from healthy contact with people, the less he consensually validated his impressions of reality. Finally, the break with reality became complete and desires were fulfilled, fears dispelled, and wishes carried out by fiat. Against this impervious wall of delusion, the buffetings of reality are futile indeed. To all intents and purposes such a solution to life's problems is irreversible. As to the near murder of the bank official, this was incidental. Of what possible import could one life, especially that of a despicable money changer, hold when measured against the altruistic magnificence of Robin's design? In the ditches alongside the glory roads of most world movers oft lie the bleached bones of innocent victims.

Why Did It Happen?

A brief psychoanalytic evaluation of Robin's underlying character structure revealed that he was a detached, resigned personality type. His "major neurotic solution" in Karen Horney's terms was the quest for independence, self-sufficiency, and freedom. His favored position in life was that of a spectator of the passing parade. He was the epitome of neutrality. His relationships with others were distant, transitory, and clumsy. He either bought friendliness for brief periods with stolen money or secluded himself. Even some of his years in prison seemed to be unconscious attempts to remove himself from the necessity of dealing intimately with others. His only meaningful companionship was the imaginary one with the ubiquitous, omnipotent, faceless old man. The burglaries Robin perpetrated were unconsciously healthy albeit socially unacceptable attempts at a more comfortable integration with his fellow creatures. His grand design for redressing the iniquities of the world represented a bizarre technique for him to rejoin the human race, and murder could very easily have taken place had obstacles been interposed. The burglaries were his sole realistic involvement with others and, to his deranged mind, justified assertions of his birthright; he was taking back only what was rightfully his. Moreover, he felt he was basically a Robin Hood robbing the rich and giving to the poor.

A mechanical defect of the pistol saved the bank official from a tragic death; the man behind the gun had been primed for murder most of his life.

Some Personal Reflections

Robin's story represented the organized summary of three interviews of about three hours each. In the first two interviews, like his fairy-tale counterpart, he proved a master of disguise, dissimulation, and elusiveness as he led me in a not-so-merry chase over hill and dale. I would feel I was on the verge of penetrating the jungle of his vagueness, of discovering the secret hiding place of his outlaw self, of finally seizing hold of his camouflaged jerkin only to find him pulling out of my grasp once more. He was a shadowy wisp always evading any capture of his essence.

The gun brought me back for a third try. During the second interview he went into a dreamlike state when describing that shiny gun. He remarked that he scratched his initials on it. He stared at his hand for long periods of time as if seeing the gun there still. It mesmerized him. It almost put me to sleep. However, when I find myself being lulled to sleep during an interview, warning signals are set off inside. I sense I am in the presence of a schizophrenic. One of my professors habitually became annoyed with the vagueness and lack of precision of a schizophrenic's thought processes. He was the soul of kindness actually but also an exceedingly intellectually precise individual. If he became irritable and impatient for no apparent reason, he would usually catch himself, reverse gears and discover he was experiencing the "black molasses" frustration of trying to follow a schizophrenic's obscure and idiosyncratic thinking. Many psychiatrists register bodily sensations such as a tension in their shoulders or backs under these circumstances. My response is to begin drifting off. I drifted off from that interview shortly thereafter but resolved to return for one last hunt after the elusive quarry.

Finally, two hours into the third interview, Robin began revealing some inviting leads. As with Robin Hood's jousting with staves with Little John, Robin seemed to have tested my mettle and assured himself I was trustworthy. I fastened on to the shadowy old man in black because he was the least wispy of Robin's characteristically wispy dramatis personae. He also kept reappearing at critical junctures in Robin's life. He represented the only latchstring to Robin's secret door in sight. So I hung on and pulled and pulled. The door suddenly swung wide, and the treasured delusional system shone forth at last.

As Arthur Miller wrote in *Death of a Salesman*, "The jungle is dark but full of diamonds. . . .One must go in to fetch a diamond out."

Postscript

Some time after these events, Quentin Reynolds' excellent biography of Judge Samuel S. Leibowitz, *Courtroom*, came to my attention. It contained a section that described Judge Leibowitz's encounter with Robin many years previously. While the name is changed to protect Robin's anonymity, the following is quoted from this section:

> One morning Judge Leibowitz looked down from the bench in amazement. A boy with cherubic features and curly golden hair, who looked about twelve, was standing there. He was Robin, and he had confessed to taking part in ten armed robberies. He was sixteen. He had started his criminal career at eight, pilfering from schoolmates. He had been in and out of reform schools half a dozen times.
>
> "Do you want a lawyer, son?" Judge Leibowitz asked.
>
> "Naw," the boy said in a surly tone. "Phooey! A lawyer wouldn't do me no good. I'm guilty, all right."
>
> "Where did you get the gun you used in these holdups?"
>
> "I found it on the sidewalk," the boy sneered.
>
> "You need a lawyer, son. I'm appointing Benjamin Spector to defend you."
>
> Attorney Spector was in the courtroom waiting to represent another client. He walked toward the lad. "Get away from me," Robin snarled. "How do I know you ain't a cop or a D.A.? I'm guilty, see, and I don't want no lawyer."
>
> "Do you know what you're facing?" Judge Leibowitz asked. "With your record you face a possible forty-year term."
>
> "Yeah? So what?" the boy said, "I'll get out some day."

After much persuasion he conferred with the attorney. Robin pleaded guilty, and following the custom of the criminal court, his case was turned over to the Probation Department. Assistant Chief Probation Officer Joseph Shelley was assigned to dig into the life history of Robin. His beautifully written report covering twenty pages was put on the Judge's desk.

Robin had been lodged in the Raymond Street jail. He had simulated suicide twice. He had written a "suicide" note saying that he wanted to die because he had just heard that his "great friend Al Capone" was mortally ill. He told other inmates at the jail to call him "Baby Face." The mature criminals at the jail laughed at the youngster and this infuriated him. It was obvious to Joe Shelley that the boy had a decided "big shot" complex. His hero was Humphrey Bogart of the films, and he tried to imitate the mannerisms and the voice of the film star. When he had appeared in court the newspapers had taken pictures of him. He had cut these out and was very proud of them.

The Essex County (New Jersey) Probation Department reported that the boy's delinquent tendencies "were nurtured in the soil of parental inadequacies." He spent much time away from home, staying with chance acquaintances he picked up. More than once he had spent the night with homosexuals. He had absolutely no abnormal sexual tendencies himself, but played the passive role with homosexuals for the sake of a night's lodging or a dollar or two. He felt no revulsions at his actions at all. To him it was merely a way of picking up movie money. He spent a great deal of time watching gangster pictures. Try as Shelley might, he couldn't find any extenuating circumstances to mitigate the guilt of the lad.

Those who came in contact with Robin had the following to say:

Sister: He was born that way.
Teacher: He is beyond reform at any stage; he is a rotter through and through.
Principal: He is a deceptive and chronic liar, the slickest-tongued fellow I ever knew. He is destined to be a notorious criminal.
Policeman: At eight years, there goes a cop killer.
Psychologist: He is a miniature gangster.
Psychiatrist: Has high intelligence quotient, but is absolutely incorrigible, beyond reclaim; he is not insane, but his moral sense is atrophied.
Post Office Inspector (who questioned him about stealing from the mails): He is a very dangerous boy and will try to shoot his way out of any difficulty; he puts on a nice act on occasions, but I wouldn't turn my back on him for anything.

Father Flanagan of Boys' Town: I will not consider taking him in under any circumstances. Boys' Town is intended for boys who are homeless and not for criminals of this type.

"On the surface," Shelley reported in his report, "the defendant seems a stable and likable person, but underneath, when studied enough, it can be seen that he is living within a world of his own in which he thinks that as a gangster he has a rendezvous with destiny. Those who have known the defendant intimately over a period of years are of the unanimous opinion that the defendant has none of the stuff of reformation. Never before have we come across so confirmed a criminal of such immature years. He has confessed to ten armed robberies and scores of burglaries. Community protection is about the only thing to be considered in imposing sentence, since all approaches on the basis of reclamation and reformation have already been tried and have failed, and since it is the considered opinion of all the people who have dealt with Robin that he is unsalvageable."

Judge Leibowitz had the boy brought to his chambers. He strutted in, puffing on a cigarette held tightly between his lips. Then, with the contemptuous gesture of the moving-picture gangster, he flicked the ashes from the cigarette onto the Judge's gown. "Well," he muttered, "what do you want now?" The Judge hoped to find some spark within him that might be fanned by decency and kindness. But he found none. The boy was stubborn, unrepentant, arrogant. With the greatest reluctance he finally had to impose sentence on the defendant.

"Robin," he said, "I sentence you to not less than twenty and not more than forty years . . ."

The boy almost tore away from the grip of the court officer. He lurched toward the bench and spat at the judge.

"I'll get you for that, you rat," he yelled, his baby face contorted with fury. "I'll be out in three months . . ."

Judge Leibowitz didn't sleep much that night. Sending a boy away for what might amount to the rest of his natural life is not something a man can do casually—and then forget. But what was the alternative?

Five years had passed. On a cold, wintry day a car drew up at the entrance to the reformatory at Elmira, New York. The motorist was soon sitting in the office of Colonel Weaver, superintendent of the institution. Colonel Weaver lifted the telephone and said, "Have Robin brought to my office." Presently a guard led in the prisoner.

"Do you recognize this man?" the Colonel asked.

"Why, he's the Judge who sent me up," he blurted out.

"That's right," Judge Leibowitz said. "You're older now. The superintendent has just told me that you've been very troublesome during the entire period and that it was only recently that you have calmed down."

"Yes, sir, I know I have not been behaving myself. I know I have been raising hell," the prisoner said.

"Well," the Judge continued, "Colonel Weaver says that you've behaved pretty well lately, and as a reward he's going to let you enter the boxing tournament. Robin, I have kept in close touch with your case through the chaplain and the prison authorities. You must realize that I had no alternative except to sentence you to twenty to forty years. The Governor always has the power to commute your sentence, if he wishes. When the time comes that you can satisfy the superintendent, the chaplain, the psychiatrist, and me that you have come to your senses, and that you are a safe risk to turn back into the community, I'll go to bat for you with the Governor and see what I can do. I want you to know that you haven't been and will not be forgotten."

And then the boy broke down and wept. It was the first time since his arrest that the hard shell he had grown had cracked. He thanked the Judge, and perhaps in that moment a criminal died and a citizen was born. Perhaps?

To the question whether the Judge's compassionate gesture to the boy of sixteen had converted a juvenile delinquent into an honest citizen at thirty years of age, the answer would have to be no. But the fault lay not in the Judge's well-intentioned humanitarianism. Rather if there be blame to be apportioned, it rests in our still limited understanding of the malignant course of some forms of schizophrenia. The Judge sensed intuitively that Robin was not at heart a hardened criminal, but instead a deeply disturbed boy. Unfortunately the "reaching" of him by the Judge's visit was not sufficient to halt or reverse the insidious reaction pattern even then growing like a cancer within Robin's mind. It was a mere brushing of fingertips, not the handclasp a schizophrenic needs, which must be developed and maintained through the vicissitudes of years of the most intense, stormy, and personally draining human relationship imaginable. Judge Leibowitz tried. It had not been enough. Had anyone else done more?

Entr'acte I

Hear now this, O foolish people, and without
understanding: which have eyes, and see not;
which have ears, and hear not.
—Jeremiah 5:21

ONCE UPON A TIME, I WAS A FRESH-FACED, BUMPTIOUS intern recently graduated from medical school. As is indigenous to that breed, I felt endowed with complete and total knowledge pertaining to any medical or surgical emergency. This cockiness was particularly evident in my enthusiasm for ambulance calls.

In the small hours of the night, I once answered a DOA (Dead on Arrival) call. It was a fairly routine matter: an old man found dead in bed in a tenement. He had been a heavy drinker for many years. There were two unusual elements, but they didn't seem particularly significant. First, he had been dead for about four days. It was only after the neighbors complained of a distinctive odor permeating the entire building that the police were called. They in turn called the

29

ambulance in order to have a physician declare him officially dead. I was the designated one and performed my professional duties—in a somewhat cursory manner. It was not the most thorough of physical examinations. In fact, it consisted of a brief glance at the corpse from the foot of the bed. When what at first appeared to be the man's white hair took on a life of its own, I realized the lately deceased was actually bald and covered with lice. There was also considerable dried vomitus on his chin and neck. I promptly decided that was as close as I wished to approach the scene. The odor alone convinced me he fitted snugly into the DOA category.

The second unusual element was that the old gentleman's wife was alive and well and still in bed with him. She had noticed that hubby had slept rather soundly for several days, but, since they had both been drinking rather heavily, she concluded he would ultimately awake, hung over as usual. For corroboration several empty whiskey bottles lay about the floor. I felt she was probably equal parts alcoholic, senile, and stupid.

I notified the medical examiner, as was routine in such cases. He inquired over the phone whether I had observed anything suspicious that would warrant his performing a postmortem examination. (Because of the shortage of personnel, it was customary to autopsy only suspicious cases of sudden death.) I assured him that in my professional opinion, that was quite unnecessary. He told me to have the body transported to the local morgue. He *might* look it over subsequently if his schedule permitted.

Having discharged my duties in such exemplary fashion, I returned to the hospital to resume the sleep of the pure of heart and mind. A few hours later the phone rang.

MEDICAL EXAMINER:

> This is Dr. Martland. Were you the intern on that DOA call at one A.M.?

DR. R.:   Yes, sir.

M.E.:   Had you noticed anything unusual at the scene, doctor?

DR. R.:   Nothing except that the deceased had been dead for several days.

M.E.: I presume because of the advanced state of mortification, you did not conduct the most thorough of examinations, doctor?

DR. R.: No, I must confess I did not.

M.E.: That thought occurred to me also, doctor.

DR. R.: Why is that, sir?

M.E.: Because if you had just raised the deceased's chin a fraction of an inch, you might have observed an incision near his ear, doctor.

DR. R.: You mean from a plastic surgeon's scalpel? Had the old man had a face lift?

M.E.: No, not exactly. The incision was somewhat lower and considerably more extensive. His throat had been slit from ear to ear, doctor.

DR. R.: Really?

M.E.: And there was one other detail you had overlooked. When the police returned to the apartment on my orders, they discovered a bloody carving knife replete with the wife's fingerprints under the mattress, doctor.

DR. R.: (Total silence. My best move of the day.)

M.E.: In the future I would suggest you keep your personal fastidiousness under better control and examine all corpses more thoroughly, *mister!*

Having been deservedly stripped of my medical degree just as I was becoming attached to it, I was unable to return to sleep for some time afterward.

Later, two reflections occurred to me. It is one thing to be awarded a medical degree; the hard part is trying to be worthy of it every day of your life. And I was reminded again, not for the last time, that the primary moral duty of every physician is to ask forgiveness.

Peter Pan

When I am pinned and wriggling on the wall,
Then how should I begin
To spit out all the butt-ends of my days and ways?
And how should I presume?
—T.S. Eliot

I N MY MEMORIES HE WILL ALWAYS REMAIN PETER PAN, incarnate. Like his fairy-tale counterpart, he was a boy who had never grown up.[1]

He was twenty-six, handsome, athletic, carefree, perennially cheerful, and utterly captivating to most women. To the state hospital psychiatrists and nurses, traditionally endowed with overly developed senses of responsibility, he was like an exhilarating breath of spring. While we plodded grimly along occasionally stubbing our toes on life's stony obstacles, Peter soared over them with his infectious good nature and intoxicating insouciance. Even his speech

---

1. "I just want always to be a little boy and to have fun."

possessed a lilting quality, a flamboyance, and a natural eloquence many of us secretly envied. One could readily picture him playing hide-and-seek with Tinker Bell among the stars on his adventurous forays out of Neverland.[2]

What was such an airy sprite doing with clipped wings in a state hospital? It seemed his Wendy also had been under age, being only fourteen at the time our story begins. And the motel where they had been flying high reposed not in Neverland but in the Commonwealth of Massachusetts, whose duly elected officials still prided themselves on their Puritan heritage. This was especially so when applied to Peters who want young girls to play house before the legally prescribed age. The classically educated magistrate at the arraignment made some disparaging references to Pan-like behavior by the accused but not of the fairy-tale genre. So it was that Peter was remanded to our hospital for psychiatric examination under pending charges of abuse of a female child.[3]

Peter was indignantly voluble concerning the shabby treatment he was receiving. He was especially aggrieved over the carelessness of an acquaintance who had arranged the rendezvous that had so incensed the legal authorities. "The only person more contemptible than a procurer," he stated, "is a stupid procurer." He also commented critically on the appalling lack of imagination on the part of police officials in not fully appreciating the manner in which such matters of the heart had perforce to be conducted. "At a time like that, who asks for a girl's birth certificate?"[4] His arguments were

---

2. "Of course . . . no one can fly unless the fairy dust has been blown on him."

3. "Now Wendy was every inch a woman, though there were not very many inches, and she peeped out of the bed-clothes."

4. "When people in our set are introduced, it is customary for them to ask each other's age, and so Wendy, who always liked to do the correct thing, asked Peter how old he was. . . . 'I don't know,' he replied uneasily, 'but I am quite young.' "

so cogent, his candor so disarming, and his Gallic reasonable-
ness so charming, one's sympathies were instantly touched.
The sheen of Peter's righteous indignation tarnished
subsequently when he let slip that he had been convicted of
the same offense four years previously, serving two years in
the penitentiary. One speculated briefly that perhaps
Lolita-like nymphets enticed our unsuspecting young man
into repetitive contretemps with officialdom. This possibility,
however, faded into insignificance before the brilliance of the
variegated and imaginative tapestry of offenses on his record.
He had previously been convicted of auto theft, three counts
of breaking and entering, violation of parole, lewd and
lascivious conduct, and carrying a gun without a permit. It was
a tribute to his beguiling manner and boyish charm, displayed
during a long series of court appearances, that he had
remained at liberty as long as he had.[5]

Peter discoursed at length and with refreshing candor on
his past life. He was born the baby of a family of eight in a
rural community. His parents and siblings were industrious
farmers of French-Canadian extraction who barely eked out a
living from the begrudging soil of Maine. "I came by my
reputation as a Mainiac honestly," he wryly if rather
unoriginally commented. His childhood years were
uneventful except for a tendency toward mischief which first
manifested itself at the age of ten and was honed steadily over
the years. Although a facile student, he was erratic and glib—
qualities that did not ultimately endear him to his teachers.
As his boyish pranks became more frequent, more elaborately
conceived, and more energetically executed, they were even
less appreciated by certain prissy authority figures. (His more
colorful description was "tight-assed.") One aged spinster
teacher was particularly incensed when her chair unexpectedly collapsed following hours of painstaking manipula-
tion by Pan. He did admit under persistent questioning that

---

5. "It is humiliating to have to confess that this conceit of Peter
was one of his most fascinating qualities. To put it with brutal
frankness, there never was a cockier boy."

the accident caused a severe compression of one of her spinal vertebrae and four months immobilization in a complete body cast, but the planning and ingenuity on his part should have been afforded more recognition, in his opinion.[6]

Peter's passion for boyish pranks persisted long after his high school chums had lost interest in joining in with him. From being the instigator of group high jinks, he progressed on a more solitary path, consisting of seductions with the merest suggestion of rape (forcing his attentions on unwilling girls in lonely sections of the woods whence they would have to find their own way home if they remained obdurate); vandalism ("It didn't really harm anyone. They all carried insurance!"); and finally, shoplifting ("If a shopkeeper can't guard his goods properly, it's his own damn fault!"). The local police authorities began taking an increasingly dim view of his youthful exuberances.[7] When blame seemed to point to Peter, repeated warnings were transmitted, though legal proof was impossible to obtain. Finally Peter felt it expedient to depart from home and hearth and seek a wider arena for his unique aptitudes.[8]

Peter related two anecdotes that appeared particularly amusing to him. One occurred during one of his infrequent visits home. His mother, aged seventy-six, was afflicted with a serious heart condition, complicated by chronic arthritis. Her arthritis was so incapacitating that she had to be carried about by other members of the family. Being a dutiful son, Peter on one occasion volunteered to drive her several miles to a

---

6.   "Off we skip like the most heartless things in the world, which is what children are, but so attractive; and we have an entirely selfish time, and then when we have need of special attention we nobly return for it, confident that we shall be rewarded instead of smacked."

7.   "The difference between him [Peter] and the other boys at such a time was that they knew it was make-believe while to him make-believe and true were exactly the same thing."

8.   " 'I don't want ever to be a man,' he said with passion. 'I want always to be a little boy and to have fun. So I ran away . . . and lived a long long time among the fairies.' "

relative's house in the dead of winter over snow-covered roads. On the way his automobile ran out of gasoline, due to an oversight on his part. It being about seven o'clock in the evening, Peter chivalrously hiked the several miles to a gas station. Upon arriving there, he by chance encountered a boyhood friend he had not seen for many years. Naturally they adjourned briefly to a neighboring roadhouse and had a few drinks. Old memories flooded back and boyish pranks were vividly and humorously recounted, if somewhat embellished by mutual confabulation. One thing led to another and his friend even arranged for two willing girls he knew in the neighborhood to join them. The conviviality was gaining momentum and plans were being formulated for the preordained and fitting climax to such a congenial encounter, when Peter suddenly remembered his mother's less-than-felicitous circumstances.[9] When Peter had heroically returned to the unheated car, it was 4 A.M. and the old lady was suffering somewhat from exposure. To be precise (although this was contrary to Peter's preferences), she was semicomatose. A physician had to be consulted and hospitalization was necessary. After several weeks of expensive and painful treatment she recovered. "I never did get back to that gal after she was all set up, too," was his succinct summary of the episode.[10]

---

9. "He [Peter] had no sense of time, and was so full of adventures that all I told you about him is only a half-penny worth of them. I suppose it was because Wendy knew this that her last words to him were these rather plaintive ones: 'You won't forget me, will you, before spring-cleaning time comes?' Of course Peter promised, and then he flew away." [And promptly forgot her.]

10. "They were sleepy; and that was the danger [in flying] for the moment they popped off, down they fell. The awful thing was that Peter thought this was funny . . . Eventually Peter would dive through the air and catch Michael just before he could strike the sea, and it was lovely the way he did it; but he always waited till the last moment, and you felt it was his cleverness that interested him and not the saving of human life."

The second incident occurred during his one brief encounter with matrimony. He had been holding down a job in a factory for over a year, the longest period of sustained employment in his life. Within a period of three months he met, courted, and married a young woman. He had been interested in country-style music for some time and had become adept enough on the guitar to secure occasional moonlighting jobs with a group of friends at roadhouses. After one such engagement he was driving home in the early morning hours accompanied by his wife. He had imbibed rather immoderately and was speeding along gaily. "I came to a railroad crossing and either didn't see the flashing red light or chose to ignore it. I can't remember which. As luck would have it, a train hit us broadside and drove us two hundred feet along the track. The car turned over several times and was completely demolished. But the damnedest thing happened! The window on my side had been half open and my butt was jammed in it right properly. There it was hanging out like a flag in the breeze. All I had suffered otherwise was a wrenched shoulder. I must have cut a ridiculous figure. Finally some men were able to pry the door apart and get me out. It really was funny when I think about it." I restrained myself as long as I could—it must have been two minutes after the completion of his narrative—while he sat with a bemused, rather wistful expression on his cherubic face. Finally, unable to contain myself any longer, I blurted out, "And your wife?" "Oh, she was killed instantly. Had I mentioned before that she was seven months pregnant?"[11]

Peter's bland mask had slipped for a fleeting instant, and I received the physical shock of being in the presence of a monster. It was the first time I understood what cold, animal terror running down one's spine really felt like. My palms

---

11. "He [Peter] often went out alone, and when he came back you were never absolutely certain whether he had had an adventure or not. He might have forgotten it so completely that he said nothing about it; and then when you went out, you found the body; and, on the other hand, he might say a great deal about it, and yet you could not find the body."

became sweaty, my face felt flushed, and an almost irresistible urge to bolt out of the room swept over me. I excused myself with as much dignity as I could muster and abruptly terminated the interview.

It was days later before I could bring myself to confront my Peter Pan again. He continued recounting the dry legal sequela of his wife's death. It had been several hours after the accident before blood specimens for alcoholic content could be taken from him. The results proved equivocal. Because drunken driving could not be proved, he suffered only revocation of his driver's license for two years and a suspended sentence for being "not without fault in a case of vehicular homicide."

Since that day I have sat for hours in the presence of many confessed murderers but never experienced a comparable horror. This was like opening a door and viewing something that forever changes one's life in some essential regard. The bland face of indifference, the total lack of empathy in a true emotional sense for any other human being, is the essence of evil. Uncontrolled rage, distorted thinking, or imbecilic clumsiness that leads to murder can somehow be encompassed by one's rational mind. Inhumanness, however, is almost impossible to fathom by one's own humanness. As George Bernard Shaw has written, "The worst sin toward our fellow creatures is not to hate them but to be indifferent to them; that's the essence of inhumanity."[12]

That day I fell from innocence. The enormous, pernicious, pervasive sickness of a psychopath was imprinted indelibly on my mind. Yet in the eyes of the law as well as psychiatry, Peter was absolutely sane—sane, but inhuman. To be inhuman is more malignant than to be insane. In former days the psychopath was termed a moral imbecile. Even this term of disparagement mitigates the true extent of the pathology.

---

12. "She [Wendy] had looked forward to thrilling talks with him [Peter] about old times, but new adventures had crowded the old ones from his mind. 'Who is Captain Hook?' he asked with interest when she spoke of the arch enemy. 'Don't you remember,' she asked, amazed, 'how you killed him and saved all our lives?' 'I forget them after I kill them,' he replied carelessly."

Hervey Cleckley's theory of an underlying semantic disorder behind the mask of sanity in his book *The Mask of Sanity* approaches the mark more closely. The true psychopath (sociopath is the official psychiatric term at present) is in a class with the brutes. He talks glibly, even fluently. He ingratiates. He entertains. He entices. He titillates. He is *never* to be relied upon. He is not to be expected to feel any of those emotions that distinguish human beings from most lower forms of life. And yet the psychopath can mouth these emotive words, parrot the phrases, imitate the conventional actions. It is animal mimicry, however, and once the crucial slip is made the whole facade crumbles and the corruption within is exposed. Such individuals know the words but not the music essential to responsible living in intimate concourse with one's fellow creatures. To some psychiatric authorities the underlying psychopathology is irreversible. To the most optimistic, psychiatric therapy is lengthy, replete with difficulties, and only rarely successful.[13]

Peter remained in the hospital the minimal period of thirty days for observation. Since no manifestations of underlying psychosis were detected by the staff, he was returned to the jurisdiction of the courts. Although relieved to be removed at last from "all those kooks," he expressed one poignant regret. He had recently discovered that there was a complete turnover every three months of the crop of young student nurses who were taking their psychiatric training at that particular state hospital. He was most desirous of inspecting one or two more "changings of the guard" so he could put his not inconsiderable heterosexually admired talents to the test once again. The hospital superintendent, on the other hand, was aware that several potential Wendys with hypertrophied

---

13. "She [Mrs. Darling] stretched out her arms for the three selfish children ... Mr. Darling woke to share her bliss ... There could not have been a lovelier sight; but there was none to see it except a little boy [Peter] who was staring in at the window. He had ecstasies innumerable that other children can never know; but he was looking through the window at the one joy [genuine feelings for others] from which he must be forever barred."

maternal instincts were only too apt to make an appearance on the scene.[14] There is something almost mystical about the affinity of nurses for male psychopaths and vice versa. The unwary, inexperienced nurse envisions such beguiling con men as unjustly maligned, much misunderstood, love-starved victims of the inequities of an unfeeling society. They are seen as worthy receptacles of her overflowering nurturing proclivities.[15] Love plus good nursing care will conquer all. And beside they are just fun-loving children at heart. Such misguided sentiment fails to appreciate what most parents soon discover during child-rearing years: A child is truly an elfin thing that beguiles and bewitches and wraps itself around your heart. But if it never grew emotionally, if it failed to develop any but the most rudimentary sense of consideration for others, one would truly have a viper at one's bosom. So it would be with Peter. He was long past the prescribed time for weaning, and the maternal breast that attempted to suckle him would have teeth marks aplenty to show for its labors.[16] The hospital superintendent, spurred perhaps by the thought of his own two nubile daughters living on the hospital grounds, expedited Peter's discharge from the hospital.

Besides, by this time Peter had somewhat worn out his welcome in the hospital. He had organized several of the less withdrawn patients into a group that disrupted the routine of the head nurse considerably. Alcohol and marijuana made their appearance for the first time on the ward. Patients had to request additional funds from home to cover their gambling losses from the card games Peter initiated. Certain

---

14. " 'He does so need a mother,' Jane said. 'Yes, I know,' Wendy admitted rather forlornly; 'no one knows it so well as I.' "

15. " 'Wendy,' he continued, in a voice that no woman has ever yet been able to resist, 'Wendy, one girl is more use than twenty boys.' "

16. " 'Come on, Tink,' he [Peter] cried, with a frightful sneer at the laws of nature; 'we don't want any silly mothers'; and he flew away."

personal objects of one patient would disappear for a time and then mysteriously reappear in a regressed patient's foot locker. Peter was most cooperative with authorities in their investigations and would on occasion even find missing objects and point out the culprit.[17] The culprits usually proclaimed their innocence and seemed frankly amazed when accused. Guilt kept shifting from one patient to another until the entire ward was in chaos. Through all the mysterious plots and counterplots, Peter was the very soul of innocence. He never deigned to dignify by his attention remarks from others about his being a "fink" and an "ass kisser." Speaking of the latter favorite anatomical preoccupation of Peter's, he did remark once that the ward seemed much livelier and more "goosed up" than it had when he first arrived. Though the finger of suspicion was never leveled at Peter (in fact he was the only patient at whom it was not leveled), it did strike the nurses as perhaps significant that all such strange goings-on vanished abruptly after Peter's discharge. In fact the head nurse, a middle-aged and happily married woman, was singularly unimpressed with Peter. "He's just another immature psychopath like all the others that come and go. And I wish he'd go before I come apart. I'd like to get back to psychiatric nursing for a change instead of this constant detective work."[18]

And so, with a last twist of his egregious butt and an airy scattering of fairy dust in the eyes of any who still gazed admiringly on his surface charm and were blind to the corruption within, Peter flew out of our lives.

The staff returned to its pedestrian coping with reality, somewhat sadder but considerably wiser. Peter Pan may remain a fantasy hero to most children. Mature adults,

---

17. "It was a sanguinary affair, and especially interesting as showing one of Peter's peculiarities, which was that in the middle of a fight, he would suddenly change sides. At the Gulch, when victory was still in the balance, sometimes leaning this way and sometimes that, he called out, 'I am Redskin today. . . .' "

18. " 'Keep back, lady, no one is going to catch me and make me a man.' "

however, have to put aside the things of a child, chief among them soaring single-mindedly over life's obstacles at the expense of those who love us.[19]

As Peter vanished in the distance you could barely make out, if you were very quiet and listened very carefully, Tinker Bell's favorite epithet directed at Peter wafting back over the wind, "You silly ass!"[20]

And So to Court

Peter had been observed for thirty days in a state hospital in Massachusetts under the Briggs Law, which mandated that anyone accused of a serious crime was automatically examined psychiatrically and a report submitted to the court concerning his mental condition. Although this procedure did not deny an accused prisoner the right to employ his own psychiatrist, the system was so highly regarded that the "battle of the experts" rarely took place. Since the state hospital's medical board was presumably objective, the courtroom adversarial proceedings, which are anathema to most psychiatrists, was avoided.

A psychopath or sociopath like Peter, although manifesting severe disturbances in his relationship with society and its sanctions, is nevertheless legally sane. He has not broken with reality nor is he suffering from a discrete mental illness. His psychopathology is usually of many years' duration and embedded in his character structure. To excuse all psychopaths from responsibility for their crimes would make a shambles of our entire legal system.

Peter was tried in court for abuse of a female child and received a moderately lengthy sentence.

---

19. "But the years came and went without bringing the careless boy; and when they met again Wendy was a married woman. Peter was no more to her than a little dust in the box in which she had kept her toys. Wendy was grown up."

20. "When people grow up they forget the way. . . .It is only the gay and innocent and heartless who can fly."

The Illness

Psychopaths manifest a "semantic disorder." They understand words as such, but emotive words such as "empathy," "compassion," "love," "veracity," "trustworthiness," and "fidelity" have no true meaning to them. These abstract concepts have little or no binding emotional force to them. They are impulse-ridden and find the restraints imposed by society intolerable and irrelevant compared to the urgency of their desires. They feel entitled to have their every wish fulfilled—to want and get what they want when they want it. Although often bright, charming, and glib, they opt for appearance at the expense of substance. Their frustration tolerance is easily exceeded and uncontrollable rage reactions can then occur.

The basic difference between neurotics and psychopaths is that neurotics internalize their emotional conflicts; they convert the anxiety arising from conflicts through the process of symbolization into neurotic symptoms such as phobias, obsessive ideas, compulsive acts, and so on. Neurotics suffer inwardly and are aware of their discomfort. Psychopaths, on the other hand, do not tolerate emotional tension but quickly transform it into some external acting out. This relieves their internal discomfort at society's expense. The acting out is usually of a destructive nature, though usually rationalized away by the psychopath as just harmless high jinks due to an excess of high spirits or joie de vivre.

For many years it was felt by most authorities that psychopaths were "moral imbeciles," suffering from a defective development of the superego or conscience. It is now thought that many of them have excessively strict superegos whose sanctions cause such inner tension that the psychopath periodically slips out from under them to gain relief in destructive behavior. Psychopaths seem to have an excessively moralistic and authoritarian approach to many life situations—but only as applied to others. They feel "entitled" to special dispensations from all such strictures.

Why Did It Happen?

Peter's basic character strucure was predominantly of the expansive or aggressive type, of the narcissistic subdivision. He identified with his idealized image and felt entitled to special consideration from life because of his self-glorification. Any doubts about his intelligence, charm, and generally admirable traits were quickly dispelled in energetic and spectacular adventures. The fact that such adventures were often at the expense of other human beings had no deterrent effect on Peter's self-congratulatory egocentricity. Peter divided the human race into two parts—one part to be victimized as he saw fit, and the other to serve the function of an admiring and appreciative audience constantly applauding his exploits.

The concept of narcissism varies among the different schools of psychoanalytic thought. Horney saw the phenomenon not as true self-love but as pretended self-love. It is a process of fraudulently expanding one's self-concept, of ballooning one's sense of importance. As is the nature of balloons, the bigger they expand, the more filled with hot air, the thinner become their skins. The narcissist becomes subject to sudden deflation by seemingly minor pinpricks. If not constantly reassured by the admiration of others, his facade crumbles, and he can turn ugly and vicious.

The myth of Narcissus did not end happily. Though fair of form and in the full bloom of youth, Narcissus pined away and finally died from the frustration of never being able to attain the reciprocated love of his own mirrored image. Self-love grounded in reality is constructive; the pretense of self-love grounded in assumed entitlements is destructive to oneself as well as to unwary bystanders. It can be fatal.

Some Personal Reflections

One of the unfortunate results of my encounter with Peter was that Barrie's delightful fairy tale will never again have quite the air of innocence and childlike ingenuousness it once had for me. It seems apparent Barrie was writing a story on two levels—on the surface a narrative of youthful exuberance and innocence; more deeply, a version of *Lord of the Flies.* The fall from innocence often has a lingering poignancy to it. I confess to certain private regrets over this chapter.

To open one's eyes to deeper truths often entails the surrender of former illusions. Pain usually accompanies this process. The rites of passage are never easy.

Entr'acte II

SHORTLY AFTER THE THROAT-SLITTING MISADVENTURE (Entr'acte I), an opportunity arose wherein to recoup my professional dignity—another ambulance call, this time double DOAs. Suspicion of foul play sprung to the fore of my sleuth's mind.

We arrived at the scene in the dead of night. The house was a decaying, boarded-up horror in the worst section of the black ghetto of an eastern city. The flashing red lights of the patrol car parked beside the curb were a reassuring sight. The ambulance driver and I sallied forth briskly and strode manfully past the patrol car. The officer inside seemed to be busy with his clipboard and radio receiver and paid us no heed. A jaded type, I presumed; had seen it all and was bereft of intellectual curiousity. I sniffed rather disdainfully—it was all so new and all such grist to my mill.

We approached the front door, to be met by a sturdy, veteran police officer with a powerful flashlight. "Where are the bodies?" I asked in tones authoritative, with visage stern and demeanor commanding. I waited for the officer to guide me. Instead, with a mischievous Irish grin, he stepped aside, handed me his flashlight, and said, "Just follow your nose, Doc!" Dauntless, I pressed on. My driver seemed to linger further to the rear than was his usual wont, or mine for that matter. I noticed for the first time that the house was in total darkness.

Upon crossing the threshold I had no need of my nose as a guide, since there was only a narrow passageway between old newspapers, cartons, and crates that reached from floor to ceiling. After a considerable distance I came to a fork, one path leading to further dark recesses and the other leading to a stairway to the second floor. By this time the officer's prophetic remarks about following my nose were making an abiding impression on me; I was being assailed by that sweetish, unmistakable odor of putrefaction. My nose and I decided to make for higher ground.

I climbed the stairs. A door was partly open and a leg protruded. Shoving the door fully open, I perceived the corpse of a black man in long johns lying face down in a pool of blood on the bathroom floor. Maggots were doing their busy work on his head and neck. Sphincters had relaxed and other such postmortem accompaniments were apparent. I felt the signs of foul play were sufficiently manifest as to obviate the necessity for any further examination. I decided against tampering with any possibly essential evidence and retreated downstairs.

I took the other path, which soon widened into an extremely cluttered living room; it was a scene lifted from *Great Expectations*. Cobwebs abounded; red silk drapes and portieres were hanging tattered and musty; and twenty-odd clocks, lamps, and assorted junk were arrayed on top of a grand piano. I passed rapidly into the kitchen. On a battered kitchen chair sat a very deceased black woman with all limbs stiffly extended. Lice were moving luxuriantly about, accompanied by the inevitable maggots. Roaches, ants, and other wee beasties were scuttling about the floor performing their housekeeping chores. Half-opened cans of moldy food lay on a table. The woman's engorged, purple tongue protruded from her gaping mouth. It seemed obvious she had been strangled to death. This was the type of case the medical examiner was paid to handle. I determined to allow him to ply his trade without further interference on my part.

I returned whence I had come. Both police officers, having good-naturedly made another ingenuous intern "pay his dues," were easily prevailed upon to reenter the house. All the windows had been closed and shuttered for some time. We opened them with considerable difficulty, improving local ecological conditions immeasurably. We surveyed the scene while awaiting the arrival of the medical examiner. A glass-enclosed cabinet held numerous rows of wood carvings. The officers invited me to pocket one as a memento of the occasion, but I refused, not from a scrupulous conscience as much as a rapidly emergent distaste for handling anything in that charnel house. A fiddle case on the piano was opened and revealed an ancient, dust-encrusted fiddle. The array of clocks and lamps had scenes of buxom women in various stages of déshabille cavorting amid pastoral scenes and pursued by determined-looking satyrs. Bric-a-brac of much tackiness lay about in such profusion that we had to proceed gingerly in all directions.

Finally the assistant medical examiner arrived. After noting the positions of the bodies, he ordered them transported to the morgue for postmortem examination. He joined us in the junk room. He was an elderly gentleman of European birth and an amateur art connoisseur. The dusty old "fiddle" immediately caught his eye. As he was fondling it reverently, he mumbled, "Probably a Stradivarius." He inspected the clocks; a few were junk but most were eighteenth- and nineteenth-century Bavarian works by known masters of porcelain. The "wood carvings" were skillfully carved antique Chinese figurines of ivory. In short, the junk room was a veritable treasure trove. We were all relieved we hadn't pocketed any little trophies in the first flush of discovery.

Weeks later the facts were finally sorted out. The old man had died weeks before his wife, of a heart attack. As frequently happens, he had probably experienced an urge to relieve himself as the coronary occlusion began and expired shortly after climbing the stairs. He had struck his head on the tiled bathroom floor, thus accounting for the pool of blood. His strangled wife? She had been blind and paralyzed from a stroke for years before her death. She died of starvation, probably while forlornly waiting for her husband to return. And last but not least, they were not even blacks but pure Caucasians in advanced stages of decay.

Some clever police and journalistic investigative work revealed that the couple had been born in Germany and had emigrated to the United States around the turn of the century. The man rapidly amassed a considerable fortune in business. In fact during the Great Depression, when the city had been in temporary financial bankruptcy, the man had floated the entire city payroll for two weeks! Rumor had it that the couple had been deeply affected by virulent anti-German feelings during World War I and had become markedly reclusive. The wife's increasing blindness accelerated the process of withdrawal, culminating in their boarding up their house for the succeeding fifteen years.

The wife had never been seen subsequently outside the house. The man had occasionally been observed leaving the house late at night to purchase food. He had apparently sold his business and supported them both on the interest from his savings. They had made frequent trips to Germany to purchase the myriads of antiques they had accumulated. Otherwise, to all intents and purposes, they had ceased to have anything further to do with the outside world.

Since the couple had been childless, an extensive search for heirs of the considerable estate was undertaken. Distant relatives kept emerging from the Black Forest of Germany for years to press their claims. The multitude of competing litigants produced a commendable state of full employment for the local legal profession for some time thereafter.

I had originally sized up the situation in that global fashion typical of the inexperienced and/or ignorant. I had impulsively rendered my judgment that they were poor, black, and dead by murder most foul. The medical examiner determined they were rich, white, and dead of natural causes.

At least I had the dead part right.

Rumpelstiltskin

The art of being wise is the art of knowing what to overlook.
—William James

HOMICIDE DETECTIVE AT A SOCIAL GATHERING ONCE expounded on the gullibility of most "civilians." After twenty years of experience with criminals of the worst types, he was all the more incredulous at the degree of näiveté he encountered among the law-abiding toward criminals. He stated dogmatically that if he drew his revolver at that moment, shot and killed his wife in clear view of everyone at the party, and then consistently denied doing so, even if legally tried and convicted, the majority of "civilians" would persistently entertain doubts as to his culpability. I felt at the time he must be exaggerating for the sake of emphasis. Then I remembered the case of the Little Man Who Wasn't There. It was shocking to realize it was ten years *after* he was convicted of second-degree murder before I was satisfied that he was a habitual liar as well as a murderer "beyond a reasonable doubt."

I have pondered this matter for some time. Perhaps the explanation comes down finally to the fact that most gently raised "good citizens" have rarely been lied to baldfacedly and categorically. Most of us operate along the lines of the axiom, "You may be deceived if you trust too much, but life demands that you trust enough." We tend to give the other the benefit of the doubt, even to the point of absurdity. Or perhaps, as my friend the detective felt, we were so enamored of the "Perry Mason" school of criminology that we accepted as an article of faith that all criminals are driven by such exigent dictates of conscience that they inevitably have to confess all, and happily so at the climactic point of a pre-trial hearing, immediately before the fade-out for the television commercial.

Ned was the only accused murderer I have examined who consistently protested his innocence. He protested it to his parish priest, to his attorney, and to myself. George Herbert's admonition in *Jacula Prudentum,* "Deceive not thy physician, confessor, nor lawyer," comes to mind. Was it sensible and in Ned's best interest to persist in deceiving even those attempting to assist and counsel him in his legal straits?

The murder for which Ned stood accused had been particularly shocking to the community. It had been senseless, profitless, and unnecessary. Above all, it had been so casual. If murders such as this could occur for such trivial reasons, how could anyone walk the streets without fear?

A red Thunderbird had been observed by several witnesses careening erratically about the Italian section of a large city. Later it was seen to ram into an automobile that was stopped at a red light. It backed up a few feet and rammed the stationary automobile twice more. At this point a young man jumped out of the passenger seat of the struck car and walked rapidly to the driver's side of the Thunderbird. The driver of the struck car proceeded around the corner to park the car and then made his way back to the scene of the accident. Meanwhile the first young man, now beside the Thunderbird, was heard by eyewitnesses to shout loudly, "I'm a police officer. You're in trouble!" He flashed some identification in a wallet and leaned over to exchange some words with the driver, who had remained seated. Suddenly a shot was fired. The police officer slumped to the ground grasping his chest. The Thunderbird sped off just as the officer's friend turned the corner. The latter had the merest glimpse of the driver's face but recovered his wits enough to memorize the last three digits of the license plate. This was immediately transmitted to the Police Department. The wounded officer was transported to the nearest hospital but was dead on arrival. The victim turned out to be a provisional police officer two weeks short of graduation from the police academy. He was also a prospective bridegroom four weeks short of his wedding.

Despite the skimpiest of information, a remarkable piece of detective work followed. Within an hour of the all-points bulletin on the radio, a lieutenant of detectives had discovered the red Thunderbird, the murder weapon, and the alleged perpetrator. The car was parked two blocks away from an Italian social club, the pistol was found hidden in the men's lavatory, and Ned was arrested playing cards in the club. He surrendered peacefully. This was quite understandable since the arresting detective lieutenant was his uncle.

During a series of psychiatric interviews, Ned consistently denied any involvement in the crime. He maintained he had been on an extended drunk with some friends throughout the period of the crime. Although two eyewitnesses had identified him in the police lineup, Ned vehemently denied the accuracy of their identification. The eyewitnesses' descriptions of the perpetrator, as reported in the newspapers, were minutely dissected by Ned. The perpetrator had an aquiline nose; Ned's was straight. The perpetrator had brown hair; Ned's was graying black. The perpetrator had a sallow complexion; Ned's was slightly olive. The perpetrator was about 180 pounds; Ned was 170 pounds. Ned's nit-picking insistence on *absolute precision* by eyewitnesses, who had only split seconds to glimpse a driver speeding off from the scene of a crime, was striking. The possibility that the newspapers could have committed journalistic errors was discounted by Ned. The eyewitnesses were unreliable, and therefore Ned was being persecuted, not prosecuted.

Other pieces of evidence, such as the fact that the Thunderbird was owned by a close friend who admitted lending it to Ned, that Ned was observed dropping keys to the Thunderbird out of the police car on the way to the station after being arrested, and that the murder weapon was found in the lavatory of the social club where Ned was apprehended were breezily dismissed as irrelevant. The eyewitnesses' accounts, that was the crucial matter. It was all a frame-up by the police, Deny, deny, deny—that was Ned's story, and he stuck to it.

Ned frustrated his attorney by refusing even to discuss a legal defense until the attorney secured bail for him. He gave assurances that he would then provide an iron-clad alibi. He refused to say another word because "I don't want to involve people without asking their permission. Once I'm out on bail I'll be able to do so. If my friends decide to testify, they might be held in jail as material witnesses. I don't want them confined any longer than necessary." This demonstration of altruistic self-sacrifice was viewed with a soupçon of skepticism by his attorney, who felt that it was more likely Ned was contemplating which of his friends were most likely to perjure themselves on his behalf.

Ned's family history revealed a divorce of his parents when he was about nine. His father had since remarried and was living in a nearby city. He was vague concerning his father's occupation. It was later ascertained that the father had been a well-known bootlegger during Prohibition and was thought to be "mob-connected" to this day. The father had also committed vehicular manslaughter recently, but seemed to have settled that charge out of court. The mother was described as a "saint," who was very religious and believed totally in Ned's innocence. He admitted that his mother had had difficulty controlling her two sons, both of whom had grown up rather tumultuously. Ned was the younger of the two. The older brother was presently serving ten years in prison for manslaughter. Ned justified this crime since a friend had entered his brother's house with a knife, a struggle had taken place, and the brother had mortally wounded the other with the victim's own knife. Ned felt strongly that a man's home is his castle, and therefore his brother took a "bum rap." It was rumored, however, that the victim might have taken umbrage at his wife's having been the object of Ned's brother's ardent attentions.

Ned was a twenty-five-year-old, married, white male of Italian extraction. He had two young daughters. He described his wife, as he did his mother, in simplistic terms as a saint and an angel who respected him, allowed him to go out every night from 11 P.M. to 3 A.M. without questioning him, took care of the children and the house, and was completely preoccupied and content with her domestic activities. He adamantly refused to let her visit him in jail, as "you don't bring an angel into hell." He stated with considerable bravado that he would rather risk electrocution as a cop-killer than plead insanity because he feared the loss of his wife's respect above all else. He had a criminal record of multiple juvenile offenses and a prison sentence for assault. He went into considerable detail about this latter offense, stating that it had been a fair fight with fists following an automobile accident. According to him, the other man threatened him with bodily harm first, and a fight ensued that led to his opponent's being detained in a hospital for treatment. He denied the other's allegation at the trial that two of Ned's confederates held him while Ned assaulted him with a pipe. Ned protested that he lost the legal battle because he was without visible means of support whereas his opponent had been gainfully employed. It was still another link in a long chain of injustices imposed on him and his relatives.

Ned had a ninth-grade education and was vague about his work history. He gave a story of "canvassing" friends and acquaintances mostly in bars and social clubs, where he would sell different lines of men's suits and household utensils. He described his income as fluctuating between $400 and $500 a week from this source. The vagueness with which he related his activities and his high standard of living raised suspicion that his main income was derived from illicit activities. In any event, Ned usually slept until late afternoon and then would drink until 3 A.M. in bars.

His mental condition was within normal limits. No evidence of psychosis nor severe neurotic traits was elicited. His intelligence appeared normal, and during the interviews he smiled easily and seemed to enjoy having this battle of wits with me. He attempted to anticipate questions and commented gratuitously on my "sharpness" in following up certain leads and trying to penetrate his vagueness. A subtle duel was being waged. I was long familiar with the techniques of thrust and parry against unconscious forces. This, however, was a different contest. Whose side was I on? I had been brought into the case by Ned's attorney, not by the prosecution. Yet here we were circling each other like opponents in some deadly game. It was a sport whose rules eluded me.

Several points of interest were revealed in Ned's personality. He admitted to frequent and puzzling feelings of loneliness even in the midst of friends and relatives. He was compulsively restless and could not stand being confined by indoor work or being at home for any prolonged period of time, even in the presence of his saintly wife. He had to keep in motion, hanging around "on the street" or in bars and social clubs. He described himself as having a strong zest for life that had never been fulfilled. When pressed he became quite vague as to exactly how to accomplish this, but he had dreams of an elaborate home complete with swimming pool, servants, and extensive grounds to ensure privacy. He admitted drinking alcohol frequently to excess but stated he became affable rather than aggressive under its influence. This evaluation, however, appeared suspect and self-serving. His main preoccupations seemed to be to respect his elders and in turn to be respected by his wife and children at all times. He evinced a deep-seated distrust and hatred for most policemen, feeling they were prone to accuse the innocent prematurely, behave arrogantly, and think they were godlike. Though initially respectful of his detective uncle who arrested him, he subsequently expressed intense resentment of this uncle's accusation and action in arresting him. He described his uncle as "putting me in the picture" as the number one suspect. He feared if he were released now from jail he might be framed by the police and killed for resisting arrest because of the victim's association with the police department. Ned's resentment of authority figures ran throughout his life. He had walked off many jobs because bosses ordered him about like a "donkey."

Consequently he had always earned his living as an entrepreneur.

He admitted to unusual ideas, such as a belief in amulets in the shape of a horn, which are guaranteed to ward off the devil. He stated that this is not unusual in Americans of Italian extraction. He sometimes wondered idly if the dead were trying to reach him but did not appear troubled by these ideas, particularly interested in pursuing them, nor to link them in any way to the alleged crime. These ideas did not seem to have reached a level of psychotic delusions: The major purpose of the magic amulets was that the wearer might be "overlooked" by people who meant him ill. He described life as being a jungle and these as being the routine precautions any sensible person would take. This theme of being overlooked is crucial to Ned's character structure. He blamed his uncle for not overlooking him as a suspect but instead putting him in the picture. Once a suspect is so designated, the police stop any further inquiries and investigations and direct all their efforts to proving they are correct in their suspicions. He stated he would rather die than give the police the satisfaction of knowing he was the guilty person.

Ned appeared to be "the little man who wasn't there." Psychoanalytically this type of character structure is known as the detached or resigned type. The freedom he cherishes has more to do with freedom *from* obligation and confinement than freedom *for* healthy achievements. This includes a desire for lack of restraint or noninvolvement, as stated in Ned's desire not to have people "bug" him and a general don't-tread-on-me approach to most situations. The resigned personality develops negative living to a fine art. He neither fights nor loves. He desires primarily to be left alone. He keeps his wants reduced to the barest minimum and expects life to be smooth, effortless, and "hassle-free." Though Ned strongly desired to be respected, this appeared to be a demand to be respected at a distance, with the irreducible minimum of demands made on his time or emotional involvement. Although he idealized women and placed them on a pedestal as saints and angels, the pedestal served to keep them at a distance rather than above him. He refused to go into any detail on his sexual adjustment. He was most secretive about seemingly minor details of his life and was rebellious toward most authority figures.

In my report to his attorney, I stated that though there was no proof or even presumptive evidence from a purely psychiatric point of view regarding his committing the alleged crime, certain conjectures presented themselves from an analysis of his character structure. Under the influence of alcohol, Ned's bland, rather affable facade would very likely crumble and his underlying hostile aggressiveness burst forth in petty, mischievous ways such as ramming another automobile that was impeding his progress. During interviews, if he was contradicted in any way, his anger would flick out suddenly and then promptly be covered over with a questionably sincere admiration for my astuteness. If verbally pinned against the wall he would become evasive. I asked Ned to imagine how he might react to the circumstances of the crime, even though by no means admitting that he was there. He reluctantly cooperated but became evasive when he felt he was revealing too much information about himself. (It is axiomatic to psychoanalysts that if a person is kept talking, even about seemingly innocuous subjects, he cannot help but reveal more and more about his personality.) Ned finally admitted that if an occupant of another car approached and accosted him while he was sitting in his car so that he could not open the door quickly, he might have felt helplessly trapped and at the other's mercy. He would feel doubly so because he was confined and because the other was outside standing while he was sitting—in a submissive physical position. This was unbearable to him. He admitted that he conceivably could then become highly agitated and do something unpredictable. That was as far as he would go in his speculation. A psychoanalytic appreciation of his deeply resigned character structure would lead to the possibility that under those circumstances he might have panicked and used a gun if one was at hand in order to remove the threat, and thus to regain his psychic safety, that is, he would have restored his "distancing machinery" to smooth operation as soon as possible. He would then flee the scene and, after hiding the murder weapon, bury his head in the sand in his usual haunt while expecting his primary neurotic "claim" (a neurotic claim is an unrealistic but firmly held demand against the world) of being "overlooked" to protect him. When this fantasied claim was not met but instead brushed aside by his uncle, he would then become so indignant at the unfair violation of this characteristic and cherished defense mechanism that he would feel unjustly persecuted, *whether he had committed the crime or not.* To him it would be essentially irrelevant whether he was guilty or not; he *should not* have been singled out so promptly on such scanty evidence. Because of this basic violation of his assumed inalienable right to be overlooked, he would feel justified in denying everything that might even remotely connect him with the crime. Such character types hold so tenaciously to this self-proclaimed sense of fair play that they often pass lie-detector tests; in fact Ned had passed two lie-detector tests with flying colors.

I rummaged around my mind attempting to get a handle on Ned's character structure, to locate the essential person behind the facade. The Grimms' fairy tale, "Rumpelstiltskin," kept intruding. I reread the brief tale and found in it twenty-seven negatives and denials. I recalled how Ned denied and denied, how far he had developed negative living, and how he denied his physician, priest, relatives, and lawyer access to his true thoughts or actions. Other minor similarities appeared. Rumpelstiltskin was a "crooked little man"; Ned was in repeated conflict with the law and was extremely self-conscious about his short stature (he usually wore lifts in his shoes) and resented being looked down upon, as in the car. Rumpelstiltskin was able to convert straw into gold while working secretly at night; Ned accomplished similar feats of magic by reaping substantial profits from the nocturnal sale of ill-defined merchandise to acquaintances.

A major similarity between Rumpelstiltskin and Ned was that both demanded absolute precision from others. Rumpelstiltskin demanded the exact identification of his unique name; Ned demanded the almost impossibly accurate identification of himself under the most difficult of visual conditions. If these criteria were not fulfilled to their exacting standards, the game should be theirs.

The other crucial similarity was the insistence on their right to be overlooked. Rumpelstiltskin contributed to his downfall by prematurely gloating around a fire that

Today I brew, tomorrow bake,
The next the young queen's child I'll take.
How good that neither man nor dame
Knows Rumpelstiltskin is my name.

The queen's messenger had by chance spied on him, reported the name to the queen, and Rumpelstiltskin was foiled. Rumpelstiltskin then flew into a rage and bleated out,

The devil told you that!
The devil told you that!

He then "stamped his foot so hard that he sank into the ground. And that was the end of him."

Rumpelstiltskin was enraged that his claim to immunity from discovery had been violated and blamed the devil rather than his own carelessness for his misfortune. He then symbolically stamped so vehemently on the ground as to disappear completely, thus fulfilling his neurotic claim to perpetual anonymity.

Ned also refused to assume responsibility for his misfortunes, relying on his amulet against the devil to protect him against all nefarious spying. He asserted his unrealistic demand to be overlooked regardless of his actual guilt or innocence. It was grossly unfair for him to have been "put in the picture," and doubly so by his own uncle. He, too, challenged his fate in order to maintain his primary principle of being overlooked; refusing to plea bargain, he insisted on a full trial and risked a possible death sentence with the flimsiest of alibis—that he was the little man who wasn't there. Predictably he declined to testify at his own trial.

One last item, a minor one to be sure. There once was a young provisional police officer who was cut down on the threshold of his manhood. He is still mourned by his family and wife-to-be. His body reposes somewhere in the ground. Ned presumes this fact will be viewed as a minor happenstance when compared to the transcendant importance of his life principle. It should be overlooked.

And So to Court

Ned refused to allow his attorney to present possible mitigating factors from the psychiatric evaluation. He said he would not give the police satisfaction by implying that they had the true perpetrator. He also felt strongly that his wife and children would forevermore lose any respect for him if the attorney so much as hinted at any mental illness. The attorney expressed his discomfort with Ned's vaunted alibi, which he had finally revealed. It consisted of several rather unsavory denizens of the demi-monde certifying that he was in their company in a tavern throughout the period of the alleged murder. Attempts by Ned's attorney to corroborate this evidence had been unsuccessful. Nevertheless the die was cast. All would ride on the alibi. The veracity of the witnesses was all the more suspect because they had come forth with their stories only several months after the well-publicized homicide. In court each stated incredibly that he hadn't thought his testimony was that important. The jury was as unconvinced as Ned's attorney. Ned was convicted of second-degree murder and sentenced to twenty-five to thirty years in prison.

Another element in this case was Ned's probable existence on the fringes of organized crime, which meant that links with other criminals might have surfaced in his testimony. This could seriously have jeopardized his longevity regardless of the outcome of the court proceedings, as it is well known that the arm of the underworld reaches inside prison walls. Ned refused to take the stand in his own defense.

As the years passed, a series of coincidences and events removed many of the irrelevancies and obfuscations from the case. First a patient I was seeing in therapy years after the trial happened to mention Ned's name. Although he had no knowledge of my former interest in Ned, he revealed that he had been a childhood friend of Ned's. He recounted that it had been common knowledge in the neighborhood, though never brought out at the trial, that Ned had been much enamored of his victim's fiancée. His attentions had apparently been repeatedly rebuffed by her. The victim had also been well known to Ned and ironically had been recommended to the police academy by the same uncle who arrested Ned. Furthermore it was rumored that Ned had stared angrily from a street corner at the victim and his companion as they were cruising through the neighborhood. He had then jumped into the Thunderbird and deliberately pursued his victim.

Eight years after Ned's trial, his father was indicted as a "hit man" for organized crime in connection with a gangland assassination in Florida.

Nine years after the trial, one of the witnesses, who had supplied Ned with an alibi, was identified in the newspapers as a member of a Mafia family, which purportedly controlled most of the state's organized crime.

Another of Ned's witnesses was recently convicted of first degree murder in the robbery of a liquor store. The victim of the crime turned out to be a cousin of the attorney who defended Ned.

Ten years after the trial and four months after his release on parole for second-degree murder, Ned was arrested with two confederates in the act of cutting through a floor to gain entrance to a jewelry store. He was remanded to prison to serve out his unexpired prison sentence in addition to this new charge. This time a silent burglar alarm activated by a TV camera alerted the police. It must have seemed grossly unfair to Ned; even a TV camera refused to overlook him.

The Illness

Ned can be classified as a psychopathic or sociopathic personality. He exhibited the classic verbal fluency, lack of moral guilt, and glib ability to rationalize away all his misadventures. He seemed almost constitutionally incapable of assuming any responsibility for his acts. Denial was a habitual defense mechanism. He also externalized his inner tensions and dissatisfactions onto any convenient circumstance or scapegoat. His impulses were poorly controlled, and his ability to profit from previous mistakes extremely limited.

The "double bookkeeping" so typical of the psychopath was very apparent; while others had to adhere strictly to the rules of the game, he alone was entitled to special privileges. Others had to be omnisciently precise in their observations of the perpetrator speeding away from the scene of the crime; Ned had the God-given right to be as vague and obscure about his whereabouts as he chose.

Finally Ned had established to his satisfaction certain immutable facts: the world was an unpredictable jungle, the powerful preyed on the weak, and authority figures were automatically unfair. Acting in accordance with these premises, as an assumed life-long victim, Ned had the inalienable right to even the odds in every way possible. The primary right to lie whenever it suited his purposes was justified because even if the authorities were accurate in one instance, they were inaccurate in so many others that it all balanced out in the end.

Why Did It Happen?

Ned's primary "neurotic solution" was resignation. He maintained the position of spectator of the passing parade, of the observer rather than the active participant in life. He chose neither to fight nor love but to remain neutral and "free" at all times. His "distancing machinery" was kept in a constantly well-oiled state, ready at a moment's notice to remove him physically or psychologically from any remotely "hassling" situation. His grandiose visions of luxurious living were just that—visions without any motivating force behind them. Life should be effortless; the big opportunity would eventually plop in his lap and be seized smoothly and without risk. All problems would thereby be solved magically.

The process of resignation had progressed to the level of shallow living. He was driven to pleasure-seeking and opportunistic adventures. The satisfactions that come from sustained and productive effort toward realistically attainable goals had long been abandoned, to be replaced with passive and fantasied wishes and expectations. The allure of gambling was increasing. It would provide final proof by means of the big win that he was indeed fortune's child, and all his previous misfortunes had been merely a testing of his true mettle. He would ultimately triumph, and the ease and smoothness with which he would assume the victor's laurels would secure forever the respect of his family and friends.

Finally, in his imagination he asserted the right to remain safe inside an invisible and impenetrable dome. "The slings and arrows of outrageous fortune" would beat futilely against this assumed shield. And the neatest trick of all was that Ned possessed a magic button by means of which he could emerge and "go forth among them" with relative impunity since at any time and any place he could disappear at will. After all, he was the little man who wasn't there and at his merest whim should be overlooked.

Some Personal Reflections

I must admit I didn't particularly like Ned. His surface charm and the "snow job" he attempted of admiring my intellectual "sharpness" in our frequent battles of wits scored few points with me. He appeared to be the most calculating liar of all the individuals described in this book.

Psychopaths are not numbered among my favorite people. Perhaps if Ned had allowed me greater access to his innermost humanness, I might have come to other conclusions. However, Ned had other considerations of a conscious as well as unconscious nature which determined otherwise. He kept me at a distance, as he did everyone else.

Ned is the only individual in this book who was probably a habitual petty criminal. He lived by standards of behavior condoned by a substratum of society but repugnant to most of us. His goals in life were unrealistic, his efforts at personal growth minimal, and his interpersonal relations guarded and self-serving.

I was left with the abiding conviction that deep down Ned was shallow.

Entr'acte III

Sometimes a cigar is just a cigar.
—Sigmund Freud

DURING MY PSYCHIATRIC RESIDENCY, A FELLOW RESIDENT, Dr. A., was describing one of his therapy sessions in a seminar presided over by a more experienced psychoanalyst. Dr. A., a native of Mexico, combined a thick accent with an almost hypnotic monotone. He was also singularly matter-of-fact and droned on endlessly, exhibiting an excessive fascination with irrelevant trivia. In short, he was exceedingly dull. On a sultry summer afternoon when most of us were suffering from post-prandial somnolence, our "evenly hovering attention," so dear to Freud's heart, had deteriorated into barely suppressed snoring. Dr. A. was rambling on interminably:

"The patient was on one of his habitual tirades against his wife. He was accusing her of constantly nagging him so that he was afraid his mind would finally snap, and he would strike

73

her. At this point the sun was shining into my eyes so I rose to close the curtains on the window. I accidentally brushed against the gun and startled him for a moment. He quickly regained his composure, however, and continued his complaints."

The supervising analyst roused himself from his stupor and interrupted half-apologetically, "I beg your pardon, Dr. A. I must have been woolgathering. Would you run through that last part again? You brushed against a gun?"

DR. A.:   I rose to close the curtains and get the sunlight out of my eyes and brushed against the gun. It startled him but only momentarily.

SUPERVISOR: How did you brush against a gun?

DR. A.:   I told you I had to close the curtains. I didn't mean to brush against it.

SUPERVISOR: I don't care whether you meant to or not.

DR. A: I'm usually more careful. It won't happen again.

SUPERVISOR: What won't happen again?

DR. A: Brushing against the gun.

SUPERVISOR: That's what I was trying to get back to. What gun?

DR. A: The gun on the desk. I must have mentioned it in previous sessions.

SUPERVISOR: No, I'm sure I would have recalled something about it if you had. You bring a gun to your office?

DR. A: No, of course not. I don't even own a gun.

SUPERVISOR: Well, how did the gun get there?

DR. A: It's the patient's gun. He brings it when he comes for therapy.

SUPERVISOR: How long has this been going on?

DR. A: How should I know? I only know how long it's been on the desk. It's been there for the past five weeks.

SUPERVISOR: What's it doing on the desk?

DR. A: I felt it was better on the desk than in his pocket.

SUPERVISOR: Yes, that may be so. But what's it doing anywhere on the premises?

DR. A: Oh, that was by mutual agreement.

SUPERVISOR: Mutual agreement about what?

DR. A: Well, some time ago the patient complained that some comments of mine had injured his feelings most grievously. He knew he was sensitive to criticism from others so he thought it necessary to bring his gun with him.

SUPERVISOR: Necessary for what?

DR. A: Necessary to protect him from having his feelings hurt again by me. I thought it was nice of him to agree to place it on the desk.

SUPERVISOR: Nice of him for what reason?

DR. A: In the interests of fair play.

SUPERVISOR: What kind of fair play?

DR. A: He felt he might hurt my feelings at times also.

SUPERVISOR: So?

DR. A: Then I might no longer want to continue our sessions.

SUPERVISOR: And then what?

DR. A: That's why each time he places the gun equidistant from both of us on the desk.

SUPERVISOR: What's the reason for that?

DR. A: That should be obvious. With this arrangement, if either of us feels it necessary to terminate the relationship, each has a fighting chance to get to the gun first. It seemed eminently reasonable to me.

SUPERVISOR: Eminently reasonable? For God's sake, why?

DR. A: Well, he was making such good progress in therapy. I was busy analyzing the symbolic significance of the gun as representing his penis. He does have such strong, repressed strivings for masculine assertiveness. I was trying to help him gain insight into this.

SUPERVISOR: You may find these arrangements eminently reasonable, but I don't. I don't even find them reasonable to supervise.

DR. A: But doesn't a gun usually symbolize a penis?

SUPERVISOR: It may symbolize a penis to him, and it may even symbolize a penis to you, but it most certainly symbolizes a gun to me. Make him

	keep it the hell out of the office. If he refuses, stop therapy immediately.
DR. A:	But doesn't the Hippocratic oath forbid abandoning a patient?
SUPERVISOR:	As far as I'm concerned the oath doesn't apply to circumstances like this. The matter is closed!

Ironically, ten years after this incident, Dr. A. shot himself to death while cleaning a rifle. He had been deeply depressed for months and had begun drinking heavily and experiencing severe professional and personal problems. No one will ever know for certain if his death was accidental or suicidal since no suicide note was found. In retrospect, Dr. A.'s underlying hopelessness about life could have contributed to his formerly cavalier acceptance of conditions in a therapy session not routinely acceptable to most physicians, Hippocrates notwithstanding.

Remember—it was Socrates who drank the hemlock. Hippocrates died in bed.

A Fishing Story

The human heart has hidden treasures
In secret kept, in silence sealed,
The thoughts, the hopes, the dreams, the pleasures
Whose charms were broken if revealed.
—Charlotte Brontë

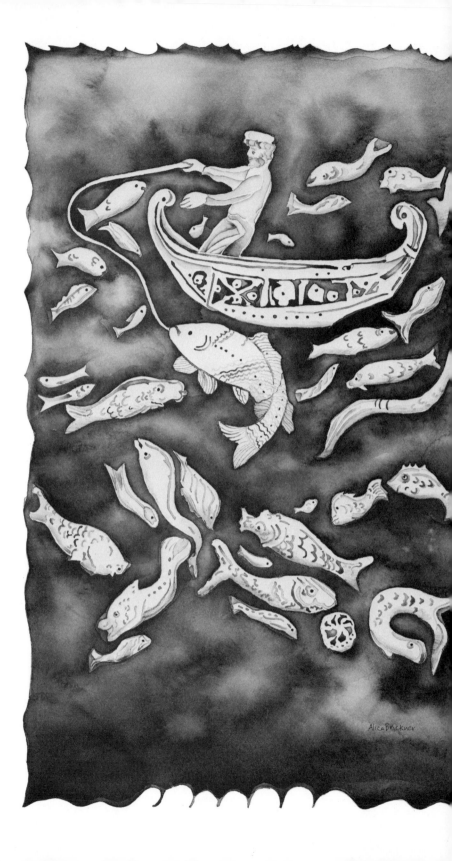

HE OFFICE HAD BEEN CLOSED FOR THE DAY AND A "Gone Fishing" notice posted on the door—the classic sign of many physicians on a lazy summer Sunday. It was the third Sunday in a row, however, and family members as well as patients were becoming restless about my unavailability. So was I, for the matter. Yet I was stubbornly fishing in the same frustrating spot in a city jail, casting repeatedly for one fish that might not be there at all, or there but too wily ever to be caught, or not a significant fish if finally hooked, or not successfully landed if hooked.

I had been lured to this spot by a few tantalizing ripples on Juan's otherwise placid surface. "It's my secret. I don't want to tell anybody. It's more important than my damned life, my secret. I have to find something out. Then I'll be happy, happy."

I was like a man possessed. At last I could understand those fishermen who seem obsessed with catching one certain fish. Did Melville's Ahab feel this same bondage toward his white whale, and Hemingway's Old Man of the Sea toward his giant marlin? There seemed a kind of inevitability about the scene. I whiled away the hot hours half-listening to Juan's meaningless droning and ruminating about the previously futile fishing expeditions. I allowed my mind to drift aimlessly with the current.

I reminisced about the information already gained. Juan was in jail awaiting trial for first-degree murder of his common-law wife, Carmelita. He had been examined for many hours by two defense psychiatrists and one state psychiatrist. They had all found him sane. After two interviews of three hours each, I was reluctantly forced to agree. The reluctance came from an intuitive sense that Juan was probably extremely ill. Unfortunately it was unprovable as yet in any court of law. In the calm, scientific atmosphere of a psychiatric seminar, such nuances of behavior and thought as had been elicited would have been given respectful attention. There was a certain paucity of thought associations, a flatness and inappropriateness of emotional display to mental content, a slight blocking of the flow of speech, a stickiness of communication, and an autistic quality to his thought processes. There was above all a persistent indifference to the legal implications of his position. He became passionately interested, even ecstatic, only when mentioning his mysterious secret—that secret he persistently, adamantly refused to share with anyone. He was intent on solving some vital riddle in total solitude.

Juan had been born and raised in Puerto Rico. The family had struggled just above the poverty level until his father died ten years previously. Juan had then come to the United States the better to support his mother and younger sisters. He had found a job as a laborer in a factory, worked steadily and uncomplainingly, and regularly sent money home. He lived alone in a small apartment, kept to himself, and had never been in trouble with the law. His landlord considered him an ideal tenant.

As the years went by, Juan's loneliness became unbearable. He was in his twenties and a healthy male with normal yearnings for companionship. One day he met Carmelita wandering about rather aimlessly in Spanish Harlem. He struck up a conversation. She seemed *simpatica.* He accompanied her to the apartment where she lived with an uncle and aunt. After a few hours' discussion, permission was granted to take Carmelita home to Connecticut as his common-law wife. It could not be termed a lengthy courtship.

Carmelita administered to Juan's needs to the best of her abilities. As time wore on, these abilities seemed more and more limited. He found himself instructing her in the most rudimentary household chores. A broom or dust cloth seemed as mystifying to her as a slide rule. She could never grasp the desirability of washing his colored socks and white shirts separately. Correcting her was not only time-consuming but increasingly expensive.

Juan fluctuated between feelings of pity for her helplessness and of rage at her persistent ineptitude. Occasional cuffings were ineffective. Once Juan even paid her plane fare back to her parents in Puerto Rico, he was so exasperated. After three weeks of the familiar loneliness, he relented and sent for her again. As compliant as a whipped puppy, she returned. They resumed their life together.

Carmelita manifested two idiosyncrasies that invariably infuriated Juan. The first was her habit of giggling. Whenever he flew into a rage over some habitual blunder of hers, she would giggle, then snicker, and ultimately burst out laughing. The more he berated her, the more uncontrollable became her laughter. He felt unmanned by her ridicule. The level of violence would then escalate rapidly.

The second idiosyncrasy was Carmelita's penchant for men. Her going price was modest to a fault—a ticket to a movie, an ice cream soda, the slightest show of kindness even from strangers and regardless of age, race, or state of personal hygiene, she would reward men in the way they seemed most to appreciate. Although Juan had never caught her *in flagrante delicto,* persistent rumors reached him from well-intentioned neighbors. (In such matters a superabundance of such neighbors seems invariable.) After months of uneasy brooding, Juan set his trap. He pretended to leave for work but instead watched the tenement from a secret vantage point. Soon Carmelita came out and kept a rendezvous with a disreputable-looking man in his sixties. Juan followed them to a Spanish-speaking movie house. From a few seats away he watched the man kiss her, fondle her breasts, and initiate other activities while Carmelita obliviously gazed at the screen. Juan could stand no more. He confronted them, shoved the other man roughly aside, and dragged Carmelita bodily home. There he administered the most severe beating he had ever meted out, blackening both her eyes. Through it all she seemed uncomprehending of any provocation on her part. She appeared more bewildered than guilty.

He determined to take her back to New York City and leave her with her relatives. She reluctantly agreed, still protesting that she was his woman alone. He took her by the arm, boarded a bus, and rode with her to the end of the bus line. He dragged her to an empty lot near a railroad trestle. They lay down on the grass. They made love. Afterward, he felt he hadn't penetrated in any meaningful sense. He was vaguely uneasy. He felt intense remorse for the beating he had given her and implored her forgiveness, which was quite uncharacteristic of him. This, too, met with uncomprehending and minimal response. Then, for some unknown reason, possibly to frighten her into changing her ways, Juan threatened to kill her. "I even placed my fingers around her neck and pressed, *but only a little.* She looked up at me and said, 'You wouldn't dare.' Then she giggled. She even snickered. She seemed about to burst out laughing. I pressed harder with my hands. I *had* to shut off that laughter. Finally, her eyes had fear in them. She realized at last I was a man. But it was too late. She went limp. I lay beside her for a while. She didn't move. I shook her, but she seemed dead. I left her and rode home. I took a bath and went to bed. I slept late and the next morning took the bus to the same place. I thought she might not be dead and would have disappeared. She was still there. I felt her, and she was cold and stiff. I crossed her hands on her chest and went to a nearby restaurant. There I called the police and told them a dead woman was in the lot by the railroad. I rode home alone."

The next day the police came to Juan's room and arrested him. It was a simple task to narrow down the suspects; Juan was known in the restaurant, he had been observed telephoning the police, and Carmelita had identification and her address in her purse. Juan seemed indifferent to the entire machinery of officialdom that followed. He readily signed a confession, led the police to the exact spot where he had left Carmelita, reconstructed the crime, and was most cooperative in identifying her body in the morgue two days later. She looked different lying naked on the slab. Her skin appeared darker in death, he remembered.

My reveries were abruptly interrupted. Something was happening. Juan impulsively stood up and crossed to the window of the interviewing room. He cracked his knuckles and flexed his shoulder muscles. The signs of tension I had come to recognize in him increased. After a few moments he seemed to relax. That ecstatic look came over his face. He stood transfixed, gazing out the window intently. It was as if he were having a beatific vision. I asked what he was thinking about *right then*. He turned to me irritably and said, "I'm not going to tell you. You wouldn't believe me. You'd think I was crazy. Why would you believe me? But I'm not crazy!"

Chastened but alert, I started casting in earnest. The ecstatic look returned. We were in the fish's feeding grounds. Absolute stillness for fifteen minutes. Then:

PLAYING THE LINE	PSYCHIATRIC EXPLANATION
Juan: "Once I find something out for certain, I'll be happy, happy."	
I: "Find something out?" (Easy does it. Just synchronize with the movement. No jerking or the fish will panic.)	When attempting to keep a skittish patient from closing off, the safest procedure is to echo his words. The most significant words are usually verbs; that's where the action is.
Juan: "I think I find out something. They not going to kill a person for nothing."	
I: (A big fish just brushed against the bait. No wonder the hook had to have time to sink to such depths. Impor-	In this context of Juan's awaiting trial for murder, "nothing" fairly shrieks for further attention.

PLAYING THE LINE	PSYCHIATRIC EXPLANATION
tant fish do not swim near the surface.) "What do you mean for doing nothing?"	
Juan: "I haven't made up my mind about something yet." *I:* "I see. What is it you're trying to make up your mind about?" (He is circling the bait. Don't move.)	Schizophrenics often seem vague and uncertain about their ruminations. The uncertainty is predominantly about whether or not to communicate their ideas; they actually have an inner conviction of the validity of the ideas.
Juan: "I don't know if the girl is dead." *I:* (So that's the shape of that fish down there.) "Really?"	Remember Juan saw her body twice at the murder scene and a third time at the morgue. Dead she was.
Juan: "Could be, but I'm not sure." *I:* (Wiggle the bait. Keep his attention focused on it.) "Why do you *think* she might not be dead?"	That damnable vagueness again. This is why schizophrenics can try one's soul.
Juan: "You'll laugh at me and say I'm crazy. It's only important for me to find out." *I:* (Laughing? No. Crying a little, maybe. He may be about to sound back to his solitary depths.) "This is no laughing matter to me. What are you puzzling about in your mind?"	The hypersensitivity of schizophrenics to possible ridicule is awesome. They'll close up like a clam if they sense the merest suggestion of ridicule in an interviewer.

PLAYING THE LINE

Juan: "Cause I seen her lots of times."
I: (Damn his grammar. If he slips away into the past, he's lost again.) "Do you still see her?"

Juan: "Yes."
I: (He's getting closer. He's nibbling at the bait.) "When was the last time?"
Juan: "This week."
I: (Set the hook gently, gently.) "Where?"

Juan: "In my cell. I can see her if I want to."
I: "Do you mean in dreams or when awake?" (Get ready to hook him.)

Juan: "Any time. I am awake and we talk."
I: (Strike! Strike!) "What do you talk about?"

Juan: "I'm not going to tell you. It's *my* secret."
I: "How does that make you

PSYCHIATRIC EXPLANATION

The timing of Juan's seeing Carmelita is crucial. If he's merely reminiscing there is no medico-legal significance.

Like a journalist, the psychiatric examiner has to find out the what, when, where, how, and why to nail down delusional systems or hallucinations. This process also shows the patient that you're interested in him and treating his ideas with respect.

Another crucial point. If Carmelita appears only in dreams, there is no legal insanity. We all reserve the right to dream crazy; it preserves our waking sanity.

The denouement. This is schizophrenia and psychosis and legal insanity. The hard part is over. Now you just have to tidy things up to make it convincing in court. The scales are weighted in Juan's favor henceforth.

He's back to his old refrain, but it's a different game now. He's opened the door and

PLAYING THE LINE	PSYCHIATRIC EXPLANATION

feel, talking to her?" (Let him run a bit. Play out the line. Now there's plenty of line and plenty of time. The hook is firmly implanted. Just don't do anything careless and snap the line.)

doesn't really want to close it again. There's no such thing as revirginization.

Juan: "How would *you* feel if you saw a person you loved very much? Happy, very happy."
I: (Well, he's finally including you in there. He realizes we're both attached to that thin but strong line.) "Yes, I'm sure I would."

For an isolated, secretive, distrustful person like Juan, finally to include one other person in his formerly closed system of thought is one of the rewards of interviewing. A little luck helps.

I: "Does she go away or stay in the cell with you?" (Let him run some more. He's beginning to circle. He must be very tired by his long, lonely fight.)
Juan: "I don't know cause people say she's dead. I saw her body in the morgue. But I see her! I still see her! I still don't believe she's dead. She tells me lots of things."
I: "She tells you lots of things?" (Just steady pressure, reeling him in.)

The interviewer can now be more assertive. He conducts the questioning instead of passively waiting for openings. He knows where he is going and merely wants more evidence. He directs the final playing out of the fish. The fish's options to slip the hook are more and more limited.

Juan: "She tells me she'll come back soon, and we'll get

PLAYING THE LINE

married by the priest. Then we'll be happy together always."
I: (I can see the fish coming to the surface. Oh, you beautiful fish!) "Does seeing her prove she's alive?"

Juan: "You're not going to catch me. I could tell you, but I don't want to. You'll say, 'This guy is crazy.' I've got no proof yet."
I: (Not catch you? You're already gaffed and half up on the boat. Your life is going to be saved in spite of yourself.) "Even if you're not sure, what do you think?"

Juan: "I'd like to see her body again. Then I'd have proof if she's dead or not. *But I see her!*"
I: "Perhaps that can be arranged. Will you let me report to the court what you've just told me?" (The last formality; photographing the prize. Others have to view it, also, in all its splendor.)

PSYCHIATRIC EXPLANATION

Juan has not only reinstituted the status quo but delusionally improved on it, legitimizing the liaison.

We're back to that schizophrenic vagueness. Brush it off, it's just a nuisance now. What he sees is what he thinks!

I had promised Juan in the first interview that if he related anything he subsequently regretted, he could reserve the right to dismiss me from the case, and I would not submit any report. This is a device used previously on patients like Juan, who are reluctant to impart their innermost thoughts. None has ever taken me up on the offer. Again, I think once the door has been open, it stays that way. (See And So To Court, where another psychiatrist confirmed these

PLAYING THE LINE	PSYCHIATRIC EXPLANATION

findings with relative speed and ease, though he had previously been utterly frustrated. Sometimes the last interviewer catches the prize because earlier ones have softened things up.)

Juan: "No. It's not important to the court. It's just important to me. It's more important than my damned life, my secret."
I: "But how will you be able to marry Carmelita if you're not alive?" (That was dirty, stringing him up like that on his own line. However, it's in a good cause.)
Juan: "I suppose you're right. You can tell the court."

This is a frequently used and effective maneuver with schizophrenics. They are often hoisted by their own petard because of the inner contradictions of their delusional systems. Their conflicting feelings are so apparent finally that you can confront them with the opposite feeling when necessary. They are very suggestible and therefore vulnerable. If one of the physician's primary moral imperatives is to treat tenderly all human meat because it is so tender, it is immeasurably more so with regard to schizophrenics, as they are so helpless to defend themselves.

I: "Thank you, Juan. Things should work out better for you from now on." (This was an exciting contest. I enjoyed it. Hope you did too, Juan. And there were no losers.)

One of the hardest lessons for the neophyte interviewer to absorb is that humanistic considerations do not auto-matically place one on the side of the angels. Inexperi-

PLAYING THE LINE

enced surgeons also have to learn to restrain their zeal to alleviate pain before they can correctly diagnose the ailment. Administering morphine prematurely may obscure the diagnosis of acute appendicitis and lead to temporary comfort but eventual peritonitis from a ruptured appendix. So, too, especially in the case of a capital crime, the rigorous and occasionally ruthless pursuit of the truth even at the cost of temporary discomfort on the part of the patient has to have the highest priority. First the truth; then the comforting.

And So to Court

Since I had examined Juan at the request of the state, the prosecutor was apprised of the findings. In accordance with the law, my report was turned over to the defense attorney. This gentleman was pleasantly surprised since the two psychiatrists he had appointed to examine Juan had adjudged him legally sane. The other state-appointed psychiatrist was informed of the contents of the famous secret and was agreeable to another examination. He quickly confirmed the presence of auditory and visual hallucinations in a schizophrenic setting. Juan's attorney very wisely refrained from calling his own psychiatrists to testify. (In most states, the reports of the state's psychiatrist have to be turned over to the defense, but the reverse is not true.) The prosecutor had no desire to oppose his own psychiatrists since he agreed with our findings. Consequently, Juan was brought before a judge in a sanity hearing rather than a murder trial. He was adjudged legally insane at that time and incapable of assisting in his own defense. He was remanded to a state mental hospital for treatment.

The consensus of opinion was that Juan's hallucinations, which were the core of his insanity, all referred to post hoc events, and therefore could not provide proof of his insanity at the time of the crime. However, such grievous psychopathology appearing ten days after the crime presupposes a markedly unstable personality who was teetering on the brink of psychosis if not actively psychotic during the commission of the murder. He recovered from his psychosis after two years of treatment. He was then tried for the murder and received a life sentence.

The Illness

Juan was a schizophrenic of the undifferentiated type. He demonstrated the Swiss psychiatrist Eugene Bleuler's classic four A's: autism, ambivalence, affective disorder, and associative disorder. The autism showed in his withdrawal, isolation, and unrealistic fantasies. His ambivalence toward Carmelita was naked: he loved and hated her without experiencing marked discomfort with these contradictory feelings. The affective disorder was manifested in an inappropriateness of emotional display to his mental content: he frequently smiled when describing gruesome events. The associative disorder appeared in the form of a paucity of verbal associations, in blocking of thoughts, and in occasional incoherence. These latter signs were somewhat obscured by his difficulty with the English language.

The aforementioned phenomena are convincing evidence to psychiatrists and psychologists of the presence of schizophrenia. In the legal arena, to persuade laymen of the seriousness of an underlying mental illness on the basis of Bleuler's four A's can prove to be an exercise in futility. To a jury, the presence of auditory and visual hallucinations (seeing and hearing the dead Carmelita) are far more convincing of legal insanity. Ironically the development of hallucinations occurs relatively late in a schizophrenic break with reality and represents an attempt at restitution or recovery from the unbearable anxiety and personality disintegration implicit in the psychotic experience. Hallucinations represent the sick mind's attempt to explain to itself and make sense out of the terrifying and confusing sensation of disorganization and fragmentation of the sense of self. Though the mind takes recourse in these obviously pathological ideas, the effect, nevertheless, is curative. The disintegrative force of the enormous anxiety generated inside the schizophrenic is allayed by the reassuring messages of the hallucinations. The psychiatric treatment of Juan, consisting of electroshock treatments and tranquilizers, assisted the forces of repression, and Juan recovered slowly but satisfactorily. This was a symptomatic recovery, however, and no true insight into his underlying character structure was attempted or attained.

Why Did It Happen?

Psychodynamically, it would appear Juan was predominantly of the expansive type. He was a "Great Provider" for his mother and sisters as well as masterful enough to take in and care for Carmelita, a waif operating on an imbecilic intellectual level, (see Postscript). The basic shallowness of his interpersonal relations was attested to by his lack of recognition of the true extent of Carmelita's defects. His neurotic pride was invested primarily in the Spanish idea of manhood, which tolerates no deviation by the woman from utter fidelity. When his physical assault and sexual penetration met with minimal response from Carmelita the day of the murder, his pride system was shattered, and he moved toward the self-effacing neurotic solution. He implored her forgiveness and confessed his need for her. This precipitous move was too unstable, and when he was rebuffed, he lunged clumsily back toward the psychic safety of his narcissistic, expansive solution by trying to impress Carmelita with his manliness by choking her. The complex situation had evoked his aggressiveness to such an extent, however, that his bluff miscarried, and he actually committed murder. He thus removed the impediment to his expansive solution and could then reconstruct, albeit in a psychotic fantasy, an even more satisfactory love relationship with Carmelita, who would now marry him in the church and make him "happy, happy." His new-found manliness was so grandiose as to render impotent all judges and juries, since *his* opinion of the validity of the hallucinations was of transcendent importance to himself alone. He was willing to go to the grave, if necessary, to preserve this image of himself unsullied by any exposure to possible ridicule or disbelief by others.

Some Personal Reflections

To some readers the metaphor of hooking and landing a fish may not fit comfortably with their preconceptions of the long-suffering, relatively inactive psychiatrist. If Juan had been in long-term therapy the approach might have been more leisurely and low-keyed, more respectful of his neurotic defenses. But when the trial date is fast approaching and one is operating near the portals of death, certain niceties cannot be observed. Time is the enemy. Mental illness discovered too late is as tragic as mental illness never discovered. Misplaced kindness on the part of the interviewer may produce fleeting comfort but years of regret for both subject and interviewer.

Above and beyond these considerations, a rigorous and even ruthless curiosity, a profound hunger for the scientific truth, a distaste for vagueness and loose ends, and a joy in the hunt for the hidden prey are often desirable in anyone who becomes involved in medico-legal work. Talented trial attorneys, I suspect, experience a similar blood lust for the chase, a killer's instinct in trying to penetrate a misleading or lying witness.

The examining psychiatrist, however, is usually struggling to penetrate *unconsciously* misleading statements in order to elicit mental pathology that the accused himself frequently wants never to reveal. The latter's neurotic pride in secrecy and fear of possible ridicule will outweigh even his basic self-preservative drives. This self-destructiveness cannot be permitted to divert the examiner from his primary duty: to discover, organize, and present succinctly to the court a lucid picture of the underlying mental condition of his subject. Anything less does a severe disservice to our system of justice, to a society of the fair-minded, to an accused entitled to excellence in his proper defense, and finally to the obligation of the psychiatrist to fulfill the highest standards of medical investigation. Careless and superficial interviewing, especially in cases of capital crimes, violates that most sacred of medical trusts passed down to us by the ancient Romans, —"Non nocere", don't harm.

Postscript

An ironic postscript to Juan's story was provided by the autopsy report on Carmelita. It revealed a cyst about the size of an orange in the frontal lobe of her brain. This probably caused her to operate on the mental level of an imbecile and produced progressive deterioration in her intellectual functioning. This finding indicates the shallowness of Juan's interpersonal relations, inasmuch as he had never recognized the degree of Carmelita's incapacity.

Carmelita's inappropriate laughter was probably due to the emotional lability (extreme, unmodulated swings of emotions) often seen in individuals with organic brain damage. Sexual promiscuity as a manifestation of defective social judgment is also commonly found. Thus, the two characteristics which provoked Juan's murderous outburst were totally beyond poor Carmelita's control.

The increased intracranial pressure due to this large brain cyst would have tended to produce death by strangulation much more easily than in a healthy individual. Juan may have been sadly accurate when he stated that he applied pressure on her neck, "but only a little."

Entr'acte IV

Why do you hate me so? I have not yet begun to help you.
—Anonymous

ANOTHER INCIDENT THAT LEFT A LASTING IMPRESSION ON me occurred to one of my closest friends, Dr. Donald Van Gordon. Shortly after World War II, Dr. Van Gordon was sitting one evening in his living quarters on the grounds of a Veterans' Administration psychiatric hospital in Texas. Without any warning the front door was flung open, and he was facing a double-barreled shotgun pointed directly at his chest. In similar circumstances some people describe their past lives flashing kaleidoscopically before their eyes. Dr. Van Gordon had only two thoughts. He fervently hoped that his wife, who was washing the dishes in the kitchen, would not come running in after the first discharge to receive the next, thus instantly orphaning their infant daughter in the nursery. And he wished he hadn't given up cigarettes the week before.

"I'm going to kill you, Van Gordon," the voice barked. "I've been planning this for a long time." Then silence, while lives hung suspended. "And I will, Van Gordon, as soon as I can get some goddam shells for this gun. You wait right here until I return." The man turned on his heel and vanished into the darkness. Dr. Van Gordon remained stunned. He sat there as if mesmerized into obeying the other's command. He said to wait right here, so I'm waiting, I'm waiting, he remembered thinking. Then his wits returned. He sprang into action and phoned the hospital's security police. Within minutes the gunman was apprehended and confined in the seclusion room of the maximum security ward. An escaped patient? No, a fellow physician in his first year of psychiatric residency. The physician was admitted to his own ward for the night and transferred as soon as possible to another hospital. The incident seemed to confirm a commonly held myth—that at many mental hospitals it is extremely difficult to distinguish the patients from the physicians. Actually this is a canard most scurrilous. Anyone who has ever worked in such institutions knows that it is easy to tell them apart because the physicians always wear their keys on their belts.

Unfortunately, three months later, while he was undergoing treatment at another hospital, the attendants relaxed their vigilance momentarily and the physician made a mad lunge for a stairway and leaped four stories to his death. He had been a shy, hypersensitive, withdrawn individual who was continuously antagonizing other hospital personnel with his exaggeratedly intense emotions and arbitrary decisions. Dr. Van Gordon had been tenderly disposed toward him and frequently performed the offices of the Good Samaritan. He had on several occasions attempted to smooth over certain petty arguments and counsel the other physician in as helpful a way as possible in order to assist his adjustment in the hospital. The latter seemed outwardly grateful for Dr. Van Gordon's interest. Apparently, however, these kindnesses threatened his shaky psychic equilibrium even more than the habitual antagonism of others, which he provoked and with which he was far more familiar. He gradually entered a schizophrenic state and underwent a "malevolent trans-formation" of feelings toward Dr. Van Gordon. A withdrawn, schizoid personality can undergo such a process and transform threateningly warm feelings into homicidal rage. The intended murderer was so preoccupied with his own intense turmoil and rage and the fantasied resolution of his inner conflict that it *never occurred to him* that his intended victim would not sit docilely by while he successfully consummated the act. He was so caught up in his inner world, in his private scenario of what he was going to do and how Dr. Van Gordon should act, that the prospective murder in reality was incidental.

Between being a Good Samaritan and a Lucky Samaritan, it is better to be lucky.

Ferdinand the Bull

*But he said unto them, except I shall see in His
hands the print of the nails, and put my
finger into the print of the nails, and thrust
my hand into His side, I will not believe.*
—John 20:25

HAT HAVE I GOT TO LOSE?" TWO SHOTS WERE THEN fired at point-blank range, and a man died within minutes. The newspapers latched on to that haunting, cynical phrase. Waves of speculation spread over the community. A killer was loose, a killer who for some unknown reason apparently possessed a hunting license for humans.

The police were charged with unusual zeal to solve the case since the victim was the brother of two members of the local police force. The license plate of the getaway car had been noted by an alert bystander. An arrest was made within a week. The mystery of the phrase "What have I got to lose?" was soon unraveled. The suspect, Arthur Robinson, had been free on bail for over a year while awaiting trial for armed assault, rape, and attempted murder (his victim had recovered eventually from a gunshot wound). Since conviction on these charges carried a possible death sentence, he considered himself invulnerable to further legal sanctions. One has, after all, but one life to give for one's crimes.

The reverberations from this crime caused bail procedures for accused capital offenders to be tightened up considerably. The impending trial was followed avidly by a concerned community.

Eyewitnesses attested to the facts of the crime. Arthur Robinson, Thomas, and a third man were casual drinking buddies. On the night of the murder, Robinson approached the other two to assist him in a holdup of a tavern. They agreed. Thomas supplied the armament: a pistol and a knife. Robinson appropriated both weapons. While the third man remained outside as the driver of the getaway car, Robinson and Thomas entered and held up a tavern. While Thomas was occupied with rifling the cash register, a patron, very much in his cups, staggered toward Robinson. He mumbled something about not being "chicken." Robinson shoved him back toward the bar, where his friends tried to restrain him. Moments later the patron broke away from his friends again and lurched toward Robinson. The famous phrase rang out, and the fatal shots were fired.

When Robinson was apprehended he initially accused Thomas of killing the patron. The lethal weapon was undeniably Thomas's. Preliminary testimony of eyewitnesses, however, definitely identified Robinson as the killer. Confronted with this evidence, Robinson finally confessed to his true role in the crime.

My involvement in the case was to conduct a psychiatric evaluation of Thomas at the request of his attorney. Thomas, as a willing participant in a felony during which a homicide occurred, also faced a possible death sentence for first-degree murder.

Thomas was twenty-five years old, the sixth of eight children of a black couple. His father was a laborer, and his mother did domestic work. None of his siblings had ever been in trouble with the law. Thomas stole a car at fourteen years of age and was sent to a reformatory. Since that time he had been convicted of thefts of automobile hubcaps, simple assault, breaking and entering, operating a motor vehicle without a license, and several other minor offenses including violation of parole. He had been in reformatories and penitentiaries most of his life since adolescence. His schooling, primarily a product of these institutions, was desultory at best and equivalent to a seventh-grade education. He had recently married, his first child being born while he was in jail awaiting this trial. His only steady work had been as a meat handler for the past year.

The initial impact of Thomas on me was an impression of brute force. He glared steadily and unblinkingly and contracted the enormous neck muscles supporting his bullet head. He looked like a bull about to "set" his horns and charge. His general muscular development was exceptional, and it was apparent he was no stranger to hard physical labor.

In his own words he described the events leading to his incarceration thus: "With two other guys, we stuck up a tavern and a guy got shot in the event. Occurred on August twenty-sixth, on a Saturday. Glenview Avenue in Center City, righthand side of street, going north. One guy didn't want to cooperate and sit down, so a guy shot him. I think he was intoxicated, myself. As I was coming around the bar after collecting the money from the cash register, the gun went off. He fell on the floor. A lady said, 'That's murder.' Guy who shot said he had nothing to lose. He was lying in the doorway so I moved him out of the door so we could get out. Robert Hill had the gun." I asked him again the name of the man with the gun and he replied, "Robert Hill. That's what I call him. Don't know if it's his real name. I've only known him three months. Fellow who was shot fell forward to Hill. Shot in the solar plexus. Blood there. Breathing pretty heavy. Don't know what happened after that. I understand body picked up at 2 A.M. Sunday. An autopsy was performed. First they took X rays. Then they cut him open like an operation. Bullet went through his internal organs. I can't exactly describe it."

It was noted that the patient was cooperative and did not attempt to withhold any factual information about the alleged crime. But there was a curious concreteness about his description. He gave a very detailed narrative of the events but without any emotional response whatsoever.

A summary of the significant psychiatric signs and symptoms revealed a paucity of thought associations, dereistic or autistic thinking, emotional blunting, withdrawal from interpersonal relations, and a formal thought disorder manifested by a marked inability to conceptualize. His antisocial activities and rebelliousness against authority figures, when added to the above symptoms, led to a diagnosis of schizophrenia. The absence of blatant hallucinations or delusions indicated that the illness or reaction type was in its early stages. I felt he was legally insane under the M'Naghten formula of the test for legal insanity, namely, that he was suffering from a defect of reason due to a disease of the mind such that he could not tell the difference between right and wrong or if he could that he did not know that what he was doing was wrong.

Extensive psychological tests by an extremely talented psychologist, Dr. Samuel B. Kutash, confirmed that Thomas had borderline intellectual functioning and an insidious thought disorder that showed concretistic thinking, tendencies to twist reality, inadequate capacity for abstraction and generalization from experience, and lack of identification or empathy with human beings. Judgment and reasoning were impaired. He had difficulty controlling aggression on an episodic basis but usually withdrew from identification with the environment. The findings were consistent with a simple schizophrenic process in an intellectually inadequate person.

The psychologist and I testified in court that Thomas was legally insane. This occurred sixteen years ago. In retrospect we may have broadened the concept of schizophrenia past the point where many psychiatrists and psychologists would have agreed. This was not an error as much as indicative of the state of the art. Thomas fit into that "gray area" between legal sanity and insanity. Competent authorities in the field would divide almost equally on the decision. Schizophrenia is often said to be not an illness but an opinion.

The key to understanding Thomas's basic modus vivendi lay in his fanatic dedication to the principles of invulnerability to time and inviolability of his life space.

His invulnerability to time was expressed in these words: "It doesn't bother me if the judge gives me 'time.' Time is

already made. Time goes on regardless. All you have to do is
live it. They can't control the time. Time cannot be described
as the basic meaning. It just goes on. Time actually exists in
your mind. If a guy takes time in prison hard, it's hard. There's
only one thing in the world, only one resource. Without it
there wouldn't be any life at all. It's water. You breathe air
from water. If you take water away from earth, nothing is
there. So when the judge gives me 'time,' there is nothing
there!" This *pars pro toto* reasoning, this regression of
thinking to denotation rather than connotation, this
concretization of thought processes is strongly indicative of
an underlying schizophrenic process.

In regard to the latter principle of inviolability of his life
space, his attitude was "Don't touch!" Thomas was an
"institutional individual," having spent almost 80 percent of
his life since fourteen years of age in reformatories, jails, and
prisons. In such institutions, because of the involuntary nature
of the incarceration, particular attention is paid to avoiding
physical contact of guards with prisoners unless absolutely
necessary. Two years before this trial, Thomas had been
touched by a prison guard for some unknown reason. He
whirled suddenly and shoved the guard down a stairway,
fracturing his arm in two places. A perceptively prescient
comment in his record stated, "In the opinion of many guards,
this prisoner is a potential murderer."

Another example related by Thomas occurred in one of his
brief periods outside an institution. "I was having a few beers
in this gin joint. I noticed a good-looking gal sitting next to
me, so I started making a play for her. Suddenly this guy comes
out of the men's room, pushes me aside, and says in a loud
voice, 'This is my woman, get lost!' I apologized meekly and
turned to go. Suddenly I pivoted and sank my fist twelve
inches into that unsuspecting bastard's stomach. He dropped
like a stone, gasping for air. I strolled casually out of the place.
But nobody would ever lay a hand on me in that bar again."

Before one of my interviews I asked a jail guard his
impression of Thomas. He said, "He's a model prisoner. He
knows jail routine well and obeys the rules. But a funny thing
happened the other day. I was escorting him to this
conference room and touched his arm lightly to prod him

along faster. He whirled in a flash with clenched fists and snarled out, 'If you ever put your hands on me again, you son of a bitch, I'll kill you.' I got a good look into those black eyes of his, and, Doc, let me tell you, I believed every word he said. I ain't about to touch him again unless I have a club in my hands!"

This same emphasis on the physical aspects of touching acted in other instances. When Thomas's wife brought his newborn son to the jail, "All I could do was see them and talk to them through the metal grille. They wouldn't let me hold my son in my arms so I still don't feel he's mine."

The most spectacular evidence of the overriding importance of this life principle was in his attitude toward Robinson. Initially he hadn't even been sure of his accomplice's name and placed little importance on the specifics of it. Secondly he still felt no animosity toward Robinson for needlessly involving him in a felony murder or even accusing him of being the triggerman. Since Robinson had never physically assaulted him, Thomas bore him no ill will. This was also due to Thomas's inability to conceptualize the abstract idea that some day in the future he might be put to death because of Robinson. He was chained to the present and lived only one day at a time. He stated categorically he would not feel anger toward the judge or jury if they convicted him, only toward the individual who actually pulled the switch to electrocute him. This is the very essence of concrete thinking. (Historically the condemned usually proffered a few coins to their executioners in the hope that they would be dispatched with a minimum of unnecessary agony. It was also symbolic of the lack of any personal animosity between the two principals in the macabre exchange.)

Once one understood this cornerstone of Thomas's neurotic character structure, the act of giving his own gun and knife to Robinson during the commission of the tavern holdup made sense. Thomas's fists were protection enough for him. He would have become murderous only at close quarters, if someone trespassed within his "lethal circle."

My initial impression of Thomas as a black Spanish fighting bull recurred. His habitual flexing of his massive neck and shoulder muscles and dilation of his nostrils reminded me of dark, immanent, primordial force. He seemed predestined to be brave in the arena—a bull of a man who would charge repetitively to the upper limits of his endurance. The well-bred fighting bull is conditioned to set his horns and charge in a predictable line at his human tormentors in the classical *corrida de toros*. A primary danger to the torero lies in allowing the bull to go on the defensive prematurely, before he is thoroughly "played out." In the preliminary testing of the bull's will to charge, the torero who is concerned about his longevity will carefully notice in which sector of the arena the bull lingers somewhat longer. It behooves the torero to position himself so as to minimize the time of the bull's occupation of this sector. If the *corrida* does not proceed properly, a bull will become discouraged by the futility of his charges, "pull in his horns," so to speak, try to get in his favorite area, and surrender the rest of the arena to his tormentor. He will then plant his feet and protect only the narrow circle he has staked out. He awaits the torero within this restricted, potentially lethal circle. To enter this area with a bull at bay, a bull who will not charge out of it but still possesses most of his strength, is dangerous in the extreme. Without the predictably straight and therefore avoidable charge, the torero, with his flimsy blade against the formidable horns, is reduced to challenging the bull's reflexes with his own. The odds are heavily weighted in the bull's favor.

So it was with Thomas. He had been tormented, betrayed, humiliated, and frustrated for too long and in too many arenas by acquaintances and authority figures with whom he could no longer cope. He had charged futilely too many times at too many elusive capes. He was psychologically at bay. He had staked out a claim to the irreducible limit of his circle of physical inviolability. From this last refuge, sudden, unpredictable, murderous rage could explode at the unwary intruder. He had surrendered the greater part of the arena to his tormentors. He admitted to preferring the stable environment of prisons to the outside world. He felt confused and limited in his ability to "size up" strangers in the outside world and to differentiate those who meant him well from those who meant him ill. Prison inmates and guards were more predictable; prisoners quickly passed the word on which of the population were dangerous, which unreliable, and which fair and reasonable. Thomas stated unequivocally that he preferred strict but fair guards who kept their proper distance to those overly friendly guards who ingratiated themselves but without warning would betray you for some minor infraction.

Finally Thomas had contracted his circle down to the circumference of his own body. Like the child's boast, "Sticks and stones may break my bones, but names will never hurt me," he defended himself only against the immediate and physical danger. Therefore he could remain indifferent to Robinson and judge and jury; the rules prevented them from laying a hand on him.

Although this Spanish fighting bull might be the image others had of him, Thomas's private fairy-tale image of himself was of Ferdinand the Bull. He admitted to having indulged an uncontrollable temper in his youth, but years of incarceration and months of solitary confinement for infractions of the rules had convinced him of the self-destructiveness of this course. Like Ferdinand, he now no longer wanted to butt heads with the other young, bullish characters, much preferring "to sit just quietly and smell the flowers." He wished for nothing so much as to be left alone. Unfortunately at times he, like Ferdinand, would inadvertently sit on a bee. The surprise of a very minor assault, such as being touched by a prison guard, sent him off into awesome displays of ferocity. When placed in an arena of real and predictable danger, such as the tavern holdup, he would be relatively harmless, surrender his offensive weapons to an accomplice, and rely on his own fists to protect his physical inviolability.

And So to Court

Thomas manifested neither bizarre delusions nor spectacularly convincing hallucinations. It was obvious that scientifically valid psychiatric testimony would have to emphasize and convince a jury of laymen that concreteness of thinking was not just a psychological nicety but of considerable and extensive import in an individual's behavior. A dispassionate reading of a report, replete with obligatory psychiatric jargon, is almost guaranteed to cause a jury to become utterly glazed and inattentive. Accordingly, the defense attorney and I wrote out a series of questions which would underline certain points which might have escaped the jury's attention. We produced a list of sixteen such questions in an approximate order which dovetailed with my written report. He planned to pose these questions on redirect examination after the assistant prosecutor, who was trying the case for the state, had cross-examined me following the reading of the report.

During the trial the assistant prosecutor asked fourteen of the prepared sixteen questions in almost the identical sequence! Needless to say the answers were rather fluently rendered, inasmuch as I had prepared the answers on cue cards in front of me. As the grilling continued, I was so taken aback by the increasingly uncanny coincidences that, without realizing it, I kept exclaiming, "That's a very good question," just before launching into a mini-lecture to the jury. After a few such exchanges the assistant prosecutor finally posed the key question about the significance of concrete thinking in determining Thomas's behavior. I fairly leaped on that one.

DR. R.:	That's another very good . . .
PROSECUTOR:	Strike that question!
DR. R.:	(Aghast at the possibility of a golden opportunity slipping away, I turned plaintively to the judge.) Your Honor, I believe I began answering that question. Isn't the ball on my side of the net now?
	The prosecutor can't interrupt me in mid-reply, can he?
JUDGE:	(Smiling in spite of himself) Court stenographer, read the record.
STENOGRAPHER:	Dr. R.—That's another very . . .
JUDGE:	You had started answering, doctor. You may continue uninterruptedly as long as you like.

As I turned to the jury their grins were all the encouragement the pedagogue-ham in me needed. The juices were flowing in earnest now.

Somewhat later another crucial question was posed. I started replying. The assistant prosecutor broke in. "Doctor, God forbid I should interrupt you ever again. I would merely like to state for the record that whenever you begin your answer with, 'That's a very good question,' I tremble." Everybody broke up on that one.

Finally the assistant prosecutor commenced posing those hypothetical questions so dear to the legal mind. The object, as I understand it, is to formulate a question incorporating as many facts and statements that favor one point of view as possible. These questions are usually so intricate and convoluted that I habitually write them out on a pad before answering. In this instance I kept staring at my notes and becoming more and more confused. Finally in genuine desperation I turned to the judge again:

DR. R.:   Your Honor, I can't seem to find a question in all this. It seems more a statement than a question.

JUDGE: Stenographer, read the record.
          (The stenographer read his notes aloud.)

JUDGE: I can't find any question either. Will the state rephrase its question?

The assistant prosecutor tried again. It seemed even more convoluted. I gazed beseechingly at my notes. I was even more at sea. Under such stressful circumstances, I resort to diagramming the sentence rapidly in order to make my way out of the morass. Finally I turned again to the judge.

DR. R.:   Your Honor, I'm afraid I can't get a handle on that question either. I can't seem to identify a verb anywhere in the major clause.

Again the court stenographer went into his act. The judge allowed as how there was an acute shortage of verbs also and advised the state to try once again.

The assistant prosecutor reembarked on his perilous voyage. He was several minutes into his question when suddenly his face flushed, his voice dropped, and the flow of words ceased abruptly. There were some moments of uncomfortable silence. Then he turned on his heel and strode out of the courtroom. We were all stunned. Finally the judge asked the other state attorneys if they wished to continue examining the witness. They replied in the negative. The judge then turned to the defense attorney for redirect examination. The latter, an attorney of vast experience and possessed of an intuitive sense of the auspicious moment, recognized a denouement when he saw one.

ATTORNEY: No further questions, your Honor.
JUDGE: It would seem as if you have been dismissed, Doctor. You may step down.

I beat a hasty retreat out of that courtroom while making a mental note not to receive so much as a parking ticket in that county for the next few years.

It is a tribute to the assistant prosecutor's resilience and fair-mindedness, that several weeks later he requested my services to examine another murder case for the state.

The trial ended with the jury's finding Thomas guilty of first-degree murder for voluntarily participating in the commission of a felony in which a homicide occurred. However, the jury apparently felt he was emotionally disturbed to such a degree as to mitigate full criminal culpability. They recommended mercy. He was sentenced to twenty years in the penitentiary.

As Ferdinand found peace under his favorite cork tree, so, too, Thomas was probably relieved to surrender the uncertainty of life "on the streets" for the familiar, more predictable privacy of a prison cell.

In a posttrial discussion, the defense attorney seemed pleased with the presentation of psychiatric and psychological formulations. I expressed gratification that he had been convinced by the testimony, as he had seemed somewhat doubtful about the significance of concrete thinking before the trial. "Oh, I didn't believe a word either of you said, Doc," he replied. "But the jury loved ya!" Attorneys can be a strange breed indeed. Their personal opinions are often irrelevant in their preoccupation with the best legal defense they can offer a client.

An irony of this case was apparent to both of us. From a purely psychological point of view, Thomas had been convicted of the wrong crime. In the scene in the tavern where a homicide actually occurred, Thomas was relatively harmless. He was far more potentially lethal in the assault on the prison guard two years before and the threatened assault on the jail guard while awaiting trial. This was the true dynamite charge that could be ignited at any time: intrusion on his physical inviolability.

Three years after this trial, Thomas's attorney reported to me that another prison guard, who had been habitually friendly to Thomas, had inadvertently grabbed his arm. Thomas, almost by reflex action, picked the guard up bodily and hurled him down two flights of stairs. The guard suffered a severe brain concussion and a fractured pelvis. He was on the critical list for several months but fortunately survived without lasting disability. Several additional years were added to Thomas's sentence.

The Illness

As described previously, a psychologist and I testified that Thomas was legally insane and suffering from an underlying schizophrenic disorder. We may have stretched the limits of schizophrenia somewhat—certainly in the opinion of some authorities. However, hewing closely to the criteria set down by Silvano Arieti in his classic book *The Interpretation of Schizophrenia*, Thomas would seem to fit snugly into the classification. The concreteness of thinking was not only striking, it was a fundamental determinant of his life-style. His basic personality makeup pivoted about this crucial defect. Concreteness of thinking accounted for the development of his guiding principles of invulnerability to time and inviolability of his life space. These were the twin pillars of his private, regal palace. When, like the blinded but still puissant Samson, Thomas in his blind frenzies shook these supporting pillars, the entire structure collapsed, heaping destruction on innocent bystanders and on himself.

Why Did It Happen?

Psychodynamically Thomas was a man at bay. Humiliated, harassed, and humbled by a lifetime of racial prejudice, economic hardship, and emotional deprivation, he had narrowed his circle of operation to the irreducible minimum. He had surrendered the remainder of life's arena to the enemy and remained walled off behind his passion for physical inviolability. All of life had been reduced to a one-sided focus on untouchability; if he could touch his newborn baby it would be his; as long as Robinson had not assaulted him physically there was no grievance between them; and the sentencing judge was powerless since he could not literally lay hands on Thomas. And as long as the prison guards did not touch him he would not kill.

As Thomas progressed through life, provoking and receiving stern retaliation from an uninterested society, his isolation from people and inner resignation from active living steadily increased. Finally he had regressed to a schizophrenic concreteness of thinking and experiencing. The price he was forced to pay for his spurious image of invulnerability was an almost total abdication of personal freedom and lasting human relationships. He preferred prison confinement in the care of strict but predictable guards to the outside world with its constant flux. It was only on those rare occasions when Thomas relaxed his wariness, permitted an apparently friendly person to draw close to him, and thus moved to a more open position of health, that he experienced intense apprehension and anxiety. He would in essence be in a situation of acute conflict. If during such hazardous moments of unfamiliar exposure he were to be touched physically, he would be precipitated into panic. Then, in his frenzy to regain asylum behind his habitual wall of inviolability, his murderous rage would explode and the innocent intruder would be in mortal danger.

The felony murder he was convicted of was legally just but psychologically incidental; the murder he was potentially capable of was probably aborted. The figure symbolizing justice is blindfolded to ensure objectivity and neutrality for all those brought before her. In Thomas's case her hooded eyes saw deep into his depths to quarantine from society the imminent murder smoldering within.

Some Personal Reflections

Along with careful examination and preparation from a psychiatric point of view, every psychiatrist who undertakes medico-legal duties needs another precious commodity: an experienced and talented trial attorney by his side. This is especially vital in his initial experiences in court. This is enemy territory, an arena in which the rules and procedures are quite unfamiliar to the medical mind. I was fortunate to be associated with attorneys Stephen Maskaleris and Hyman Isaac in my first baptisms under fire. Those cases developed into amicable legal confrontations. Having been initiated in such relatively painless fashion, a more deadly conflict such as in this case could be handled with equanimity. If a neophyte psychiatric witness is "roughed up" and professionally embarrassed in his first legal outings, he is apt to avoid any repetition by refusing future assignments. Once he is familiar with the basic ground rules (which customarily permit considerable latitude and avoidance of the strictures of a yes or no answer by the "expert witness," as opposed to the material witness), court appearances can be approached more as a forum to instruct the jury about the essential psychopathology relevant to the case than as an exercise in adversarial confrontation.

Being a bit of a ham also helps.

Postscript

Eighteen years after Thomas's trial, his defense attorney relayed this incident. He noticed something familiar about a man depositing considerable amounts of cash and checks into a commercial account at the bank he habitually used. He must have been staring somewhat, as the other man turned to him and said, "Counselor, you may not be able to place me, but I'm Arthur Robinson. I've been out of prison for several years. I'm working steady and am entrusted with my company's weekly receipts. So don't be nervous. I'm only a murderer, not a bank robber. Your money is safe here." Robinson then laughed gaily and strode out of the bank.

Ironically, it was subsequently learned that although Robinson was back in the community, Thomas was still confined in prison. Thomas has spent much of these intervening years in solitary confinement due to unpredictable assaultiveness and repeated rebelliousness against authorities. One wonders whether the outcome would have been different if he had been recognized and treated as a schizophrenic.

My Ferdinand has not yet been able to find and sit "under his favorite cork tree, smelling the flowers just quietly." Perhaps someday he will.

Entr'acte V

Good name in man and woman, dear my lord,
Is the immediate jewel of their souls:
Who steals my purse steals trash; 'tis something, nothing;
'Twas mine, 'tis his, and has been slave to thousands;
But he that filches from me my good name
Robs me of that which not enriches him,
And makes me poor indeed.
—Othello III, iii

THEN, THERE IS THE ONLY OCCASION ON WHICH I WAS accused of murder.

I had previously published a scientific paper on murder, and many of my patients were aware of my special interest in the subject. One patient, Bob, had been in therapy for about two years. He was a delightful young man: charming, well mannered, habitually calm, always punctual, and cooperative to the best of his ability—a nice young man—so nice that we were getting nowhere in therapy. He was also a homosexual with considerable guilt over his sexuality.

One Saturday morning he was driving toward my office-home for an 8 A.M. appointment. Over his car radio came a news bulletin: "Dr. Ruvolo [I pronounce my name 'Rutolo,' Italian purism notwithstanding], an anesthetist at St. Eliza-

121

beth's Hospital in Elizabeth [a town adjoining mine] has run amok in the parking lot of the hospital. He has shot and killed a fellow physician and wounded a bystander. He has been apprehended and is in protective custody awaiting psychiatric evaluation." Bob kept driving along and thought to himself: "My friends were right after all. Whenever I mentioned being in psychoanalysis, they said all shrinks were crazy themselves. So mine finally flipped. I knew his hobby was murders, but this is ridiculous. Strange, though . . . I thought his practice was quite successful. I must have been wrong there, too. He apparently has had to moonlight as an anesthetist to make ends meet. Next thing I know he'll be raising my fee!"

He proceeded placidly along while allowing these thoughts to pass through his mind. He arrived at my office, rang the bell, and tried to enter as was customary. The door was locked! As luck would have it, I had overslept. Bob suddenly realized the significance of the locked door. "That was stupid of me. It had completely slipped my mind that the news report said Dr. Ruotolo was in protective custody." He turned slowly about and returned to his car. By this time the doorbell's ringing had awakened me. I leaned out the bedroom window, which was directly above the office waiting room, and told him that I would be down shortly. Bob looked up blandly and waited. A few minutes later, I admitted him. The session proceeded as did most other sessions with Bob: the blind leading the bland. No mention of the news bulletin was made.

Several months later I happened to remark to Bob that a Dr. Ruvolo had just been arraigned in a local court and declared insane. I had taken considerable kidding from friends because of the obvious similarity of names. Bob laughed politely and then related his previously subliminal ruminations. He hadn't thought them particularly noteworthy. He was mildly surprised that I seemed interested in exploring his idle thoughts at some length. It soon developed that the main reason he had not thought it appropriate to discuss these fantasies was that for most of his life he had been secretly convinced that *all* "straight" males were basically potential murderers. The only questions of concern to him were when would they explode, and would he be in the line of fire?

This represented the watershed of Bob's psychoanalysis. At last, true therapy could commence. The mask of blandness could finally be removed, and his deep-seated fears of aggressiveness from others, especially males, could be touched, shared, and worked through. The polite surface probing was over forever, and serious grappling with his inner lifelong terror could occur.

Needless to say, as a proper, all-accepting therapist I soon forgot Bob's accusing me of murder. It took considerably longer to forgive the moonlighting charge. It's all a matter of where you invest your neurotic pride.

The Pied Piper

*I deal with the only subject worthy of a writer:
the problems of the human heart in conflict with itself.*
—William Faulkner

O THE BEST OF MY RECOLLECTION I WAS JUST CRUISING in my dump truck. The company expects us drivers to take the trucks home nights to prevent them from being ripped off at the work site. I had been drinking hard for three days. I seen Eloise walking along alone. She being only about six, I offered her a ride home. She jumped into the cab. A look passed between us, but no words were spoken. It was her special look.[1]

---

1. "I'm able
By means of a secret charm, to draw
All creatures living beneath the sun,
That creep or swim or fly or run,
After me so as you never saw!"

127

"I had to pull over to the curb because I felt woozy. Happened three times. Passed out each time. Eloise waited patiently till I come to. It started getting dark. Next thing I remember we were in my apartment. I started undressing her. She said nothing. I had sex with her vaginally and rectally. Don't think she screamed or anything. Afterwards she looked up at me in a certain way and asked quietly, 'Now can I go home?'

"Something exploded inside my head. I realized what I had done. I felt terrified. Placed my hands over her nose and mouth. Her eyes became glassy. She went limp. I remembered noticing it started raining about then. I dressed her and placed her body in my closet.

"I couldn't go near that closet for days. I kept drinking steady. After four days I placed Eloise's body in the truck after dark. I drove around for hours. Finally arrived at my job site. The company was dumping tons of dirt as fill in a marshy area near an airport. Nobody was around. I thought of burying her there where nobody would ever discover her.[2] I couldn't do it. After many more hours of driving, I stopped by a cemetery. I placed her body inside the gate wrapped in one of my blankets so she'd at least get a Christian buryin'. I left her lying there in the rain.

"I thought several times of telling my girl friend what I done but always stopped just short.

"Some weeks later I was baby-sitting my brother's kids. His wife had a six-year-old daughter, Iris, from a previous marriage. While Iris was asleep, I started taking my trousers off. Suddenly I caught myself and ran from the apartment. I was really scared. Went to a bar and drank myself into stupefaction.

"The next week I broke into my company's offices and took some office equipment and some checks. When I tried to cash

---

2.   "When, lo as they reached the mountain side
A wondrous portal opened wide
As if a cavern was suddenly hollowed;
And the Piper advanced and the children followed,
And when all were in to the very last,
The door in the mountain side shut fast."

the checks, I used my own identification. In the middle of the transaction, I panicked and ran. The police picked me up, but my employers wouldn't press charges. They said I was a good worker and had never done nothin' like that before.[3] What I couldn't understand was why I did those things and especially then? I was working double shifts regular and had more than enough money. I never broke into places before in my life.

"Then my brother's wife was told by Iris about my exposing myself. Iris hadn't been asleep after all. The wife blew her top and pressed charges against me. While in jail on this charge, the police questioned me about Eloise's disappearance. I told them all about it. It was a relief to get it off my mind at last.

"What was my raisin' like? I was raised by a pappy and mammy who both drank heavy most of the time. They fought often and once mammy cut pappy with a knife about the face. She ran out, leaving me and my younger brother with him bleeding all over the kitchen. We called the police. I dream about it often.

"Pappy took off when I was about ten. He never sent no support money so mammy worked mostly. Now I run into him occasionally. We have a few drinks together. He ain't much good, though, and I worry that I'll turn out an old drunk like him. I get touchy and fly into rages with him and fear that I might hurt him someday.

" 'Cause we never had 'nough money, we had to live in the most God-awful tenements. Real rattraps they were.[4] Matter of fact, me and my brother were always setting traps for rats but never seemed to get ahead of them. I'd get specially angry when I heard of cases where rats killed babies in their cribs. Rats—I can't stand them to this day. I'll grab a broom or anything and go wild trying to kill them whenever I see one.

---

3. "And I chiefly use my charm
On creatures that do people harm,
The mole and toad and newt and viper;
And people call me the Pied Piper."

4. "Rats!
They fought the dogs and killed the cats,
And bit the babies in the cradles. . ."

I'd like to drown every rat on earth—that's the best way to get rid of them![5]

"I done all right in school till the ninth grade. Then I kinda lost interest. Started playing hooky and finally quit altogether. Joined the marine corps and served in Vietnam. Didn't see much action except in court-martials for giving sergeants back some of their shit. Finally given a general discharge. I couldn't stand that spit and polish and everyone ordering you around all the time.

"I been living with my mammy mostly and working double shifts as a truck driver. I gets restless hanging around the house too much. Have to be on the move constantly.[6] I been drinking heavier lately. Had five minor accidents while under the influence but managed to hold on to my license.

"Sexual experiences? I get it regular from girl friends. Prefer black girls, don't want to mess with no white folks. I perform okay except for some straining and pushing just before climaxing. I like it better if I'm forcing the gal against her will. I'm no rapo though. Never had no need for that. If the gal were pregnant with my child I liked it most of all. A few times I've had to cuff a gal some, and I seem to like sex more afterwards. Lately I've been amazed to find I can enjoy intercouse even more if I relax and don't push so hard. . . . Sooner or later though it seems as if I have to hurt those I love.

"Never had no trouble with the law till recently. Fact, coincidental with my arrest for exposing myself to Iris, I had been considering killing my mammy's half-sister with some scissors. She usually sided with me if I had an argument with others in the family. But for some reason I figured her to be two-faced and untrustworthy. I really was thinking on killing her. . . . Can't recollect why now.

------

5. "Anything like the sound of a rat
Makes my heart go pit-a-pat!"

6. "The Piper's face fell, and he cried,
'No trifling! I can't wait, beside!
I've promised to visit by dinner time
Bagdad . . .' "

"No, I never had any childhood fears except for one. Never could stand water. Scared me silly.[7] Going overseas with the marines I couldn't sleep a wink on board ship. Mammy used to send me and my brother to the city pool to learn to swim. We'd make up a fib and use the money to go to the movies. Speaking of that, it was strange that it always seems to be raining at bad times in my life. It rained the night I killed Eloise, and when I placed her body in the cemetery, and when I almost assaulted Iris, and the night I felt like killing mammy's half-sister.

"Oh, and one other time it was raining. I had this dream, see, in which I shot a stranger to death in a tavern while it was raining. We were both in marine uniforms, so it must have been in San Diego, California. I know 'cause I only wore that uniform in the States after returning from Asia and was discharged from the service in San Diego. The dream was so real I was sure it must have been a memory of a true event. It has bothered me so much I had my attorney call California to find out if there were any unsolved murders during the time I was there. He did so and said there were none. I'm still not completely sure, though.

"Any other strange or mystical events ever happened to me? Well, as a matter of fact there is one. In the past few years I've noticed something strange that's happened six or eight times. Two or more black dudes will suddenly stare at me, snap their fingers, and look upwards. Four of these incidents have taken place here in jail. When it happens I become terrified. I'm afraid to look upwards, as some catastrophe might occur if I did so. Whenever these dudes drop a stare on me, I break out into a cold sweat.[8] Once or twice I was afeared you was in with them, Doc, as you look upwards at times. You

---

7. "Just as methought it said, 'Come, bore me!'
— I found the [River] Weser rolling o'er me."

8. "The music stopped and I stood still,
And found myself outside the hill,
Left alone against my will,
To go now limping as before,
And never hear of that [imaginary] country more!"

never snap your fingers, though. I don't know for sure—these dudes might be operating as a group to control me. Or they might want me to join their group in order to accomplish something or other important. I do think I may have been put on earth to accomplish something better than to have killed Eloise.

"Another time I woke up in my cell to see a crucifix on the wall. It wasn't there for long. I figured it meant everything was going to be all right, whether I got the electric chair or not. I felt it was a direct message from God. It gave me a good feeling. Never had it before. It seemed to mean I was special and things would turn out all right regardless of what happens.

"I have feelings of recognizing places where I couldn't possibly have been before. I wonder if that means I've been in another life and perhaps am still there.[9] I told myself I'm ready to go back to this other life. These feelings come to me when I'm alone in a bar. The whole scene will suddenly seem familiar, and I can sense just what's going to happen next. I drink to forget it. I worry about that more on the street than in jail. I wonder sometimes if it means I might be going crazy.

"What do I think about kids? The thing I wanted more than anything in the world was to have kids of my own!'"

Here he broke down into uncontrollable sobs. It was the most dramatic display of feeling in all the hours of interviewing. After five minutes he brought himself under control again.

---

9. ". . . in Transylvania there's a tribe
Of alien people that ascribe
The outlandish ways and dress
On which their neighbours lay such stress,
To their fathers and mothers having risen
Out of some subterraneous prison
Into which they were trepanned
Long time ago in a mighty band
Out of Hamelin town in Brunswick land,
But how or why, they don't understand."

"One gal had an abortion from a pregnancy I caused before I found out about it. I broke off with her over it. Then my last girl friend, who was separated from her husband, got pregnant by me. She said she'd lose custody of her other kids and possibly her welfare check if she was found to be pregnant illegitimately. I told her I would shoot myself in front of her and let myself bleed to death unless she promised not to have the abortion. When I confronted her, she had already gotten rid of it. I can't understand those black folks who think of a kid as just another damn mouth to feed. Every kid deserves a chance to live. Friends and relatives always told me I had a knack with kids. Kids always adored me, and I them. I used to love to play my harmonica for them and give them candy and pop. They used to follow me all over the neighborhood. They loved to ride in the back of my truck. I was known as the black Pied Piper."[10]

The pattern of the typical child molester was shattered by his next remarks.

"I had this snapshot of Eloise with me all through my marine corps tour of duty. First it was of her at two years of age. Later I had one of her a little older. My buddies in the marines thought she was my daughter. I never told them she wasn't. Her pictures were the only ones I carried. The night Eloise disappeared, her relatives asked me if I knew where she was as she was so crazy about me she hung around me whenever she could. . . . There was something different about Eloise. She'd look up at me in a certain way. I'd look down at her. Nothing would be said. It was just a look, but it stood out from all the others. . . . It was as if she was expecting me to do

---

10. "Out came the children running.
All the little boys and girls,
With rosy cheeks and flaxen curls,
And sparkling eyes and teeth like pearls,
Tripping and skipping, ran merrily after
The wonderful music with shouting and laughter."

something for her or show her something.[11] I used to wonder if it was because she had never had a pappy. Something in her eyes seemed to want something of me. I'd see that look on occasion in my stepniece's eyes, too, the one I almost had sex with . . . It's funny but both Eloise and Iris used to tell everyone that they wanted to grow up as fast as possible so they could marry me. I had never thought of that coincidence before.[12]

"From age fifteen on I used to have this vague premonition that something bad would happen to me that I couldn't prevent. Maybe some crime while drinking . . . *But the least likely crime that I ever thought about was harming kids!* 'Cause I was crazy about kids, all kids, but especially Eloise. But after you kill a kid, you can hardly be crazy about them, can you? Tell me, Doc, have I always really liked kids, or was it all false, and I really hated them?"

He broke down into deep, racking sobs again.

And So to Court

The psychiatric findings were presented to the prosecuting attorney, who agreed fundamentally and accepted a plea of guilty of second-degree murder and a life sentence. Six weeks after sentencing, Otto was suddenly transferred from the state prison to the state mental hospital because of psychotic

---

11. ". . . The Piper also promised me,
For he led us, he said, to a joyous land,
Joining the town and just at hand,
Where waters gushed and fruit trees grew,
And flowers put forth a fairer hue,
And everything was strange and new; . . . .
And honey-bees had lost their stings,
And horses were born with eagles' wings."

12. "Into the street the Piper stept,
Smiling first a little smile,
As if he knew what magic slept
In his quiet pipe the while . . ."

behavior of a schizo-affective type. He recovered in three months with rest and medication.

I interviewed Otto in the state prison several weeks after his recovery. As is common among individuals following psychotic breaks with reality, Otto was exceedingly reluctant to discuss his recent mental illness. He denied any visions of supernatural events connected with people snapping their fingers and looking upwards. However, his denials had a somewhat hollow ring—as if he might have experienced something in this regard which he preferred to forget. Since the tranquilizers and antidepressants he had received were designed to assist this process of recovery by the repression of frightening ideas, I felt humanitarian considerations took precedence over scientific curiosity. Accordingly I did not pursue this line of inquiry zealously. The suspicion remains that Otto's timing was somewhat off, as far as a medico-legal defense of insanity was concerned. In contrast to Juan of the Fishing Story, Otto's insanity occurred *after* rather than *before* sentencing.

As Hesiod said, "Observe due measure, for right timing is in all things the most important factor" [*Works and Days,* 1. 694].

The Illness

The psychiatric diagnosis seemed to rest between sociopathic personality disorder with alcoholism and without psychosis and a borderline character disorder. (By the latter diagnosis is meant a person who is sicker than a neurotic, who internalizes his symptoms, but who is not quite sick enough to be classified as overtly psychotic—having broken with reality—and therefore legally insane.) Otto was, however, exceedingly close to fulfilling the criteria for legal insanity under the M'Naghten rule. He had experienced at least one visual hallucination, had considered suicide several times, was confused and terrified about whether a dream represented reality or fantasy, and had had frequent déjà vu phenomena toward which his emotional attitude was quite disturbed. Further, he might have been incubating a paranoid delusional system regarding the group of men who could have been out to control his mind. This latter symptom is among the most ominous signs of a deeply disturbed mental state. However, there was no description of his having acted on these pathological ideas nor did they appear connected in any intimate way with his alleged crime. In the legal sense of insanity, delusional ideas have to be connected with the actual crime for which the person is being tried. Ironically, Otto probably was deteriorating mentally, as shown by the outbreak of thoughts and impulses to kill his aunt with minimal provocation shortly before his arrest. As a result of his confinement in jail his mental condition improved somewhat, as he did not feel as threatened by the people about him and therefore appeared healthier than he might otherwise. He indicated this by stating that if he were released at the present time without being punished for the murder of Eloise, he would immediately sign himself into a mental hospital for treatment because "there must be something wrong with my head for me to have done what I did." He also seriously considered committing suicide if it were not possible for him to receive treatment.

Why Did It Happen?

Psychodynamically Otto was a very immature, anxious young man who had always felt a close affinity for children and identified himself with them, especially with their silent yearning for adult affection and protection. He particularly empathized with unwanted children, as shown by his intense emotional response to abortions. Although he struggled to appear manly through his enlistment in the marine corps, his feats of drinking, his sexual prowess, and his petty thievery, he actually experienced himself as inadequate in the adult world. His self-hate was so enormous he could never really trust adults' approval and constantly and repetitively hurt those he loved. He lied to his mother, fought with his father, thought of killing his aunt, and experienced a heightened enjoyment of sex with adult women, particularly if he were hurting them before or during the sexual act. With adult women he was always pressing too hard, both literally and figuratively, to disguise his shrunken, self-effacing self-image. His constant state of anxiety was handled chiefly by using alcohol as a narcotizing agent. He was deeply alienated from his own inner feelings of both affection and hostility. His immature, erratic, and clumsily affectionate impulses, when released by excessive alcoholic intake, finally broke through in a single act of carnal abuse of his fantasied daughter, Eloise. It would appear that after the act, the full realization of the inevitable consequences struck him, and he panicked and choked her to death. The speculation presents itself that the murderous impulse might not have broken out if Eloise had not quietly said, "Now can I go home?" The state of enormous self-hate in which he was immersed was probably intensified by the child's too-calm acceptance of that which was completely unacceptable to him. For instance, if she had cried and asked for his immediate help in making up an elaborate excuse for her absence to her mother, Otto might have been able to reinstitute his former neurotic pride in his role of child protector and to allay his own panic. Instead, his self-hate, unbound and unconfronted, exploded.

The underlying shock after the rape was due not only to his abhorrence of the sexual crime as society would view it, but to a total undermining of his basic neurotic pride system and his idealized image of himself: that of the benevolent, ever-reliable, utterly selfless child protector. This sexual act pre-cipitated in him a catastrophic conflict accompanied by over-whelming panic. In place of his long-cherished role of the child protector, he suddenly became the despicable child molester. Instead of his glorified image he confronted his unconscious self-hate ("Have I always really hated children?"), the shadow of his neurotic pride. The panic that ensued in finding himself in this inconceivable position of child molester made him lurch back to his former psychic position of child protector by removing, through murder, the only living symbol which prevented the reestablishment of that image: the unfortunate Eloise.

From child protector he had passed to child molester. From this unbearable position he became the child murderer in order to return to the child protector, if only the dead-child protector. Once that final act had been accomplished, he *had* to place her body in the closet and couldn't bear to approach it for almost a week. When finally he did attempt to dispose of the body, instead of burying it under tons of dirt at his work site, where in all probability it would never have been discovered, the reestablishment of his child-protector role demanded from him an altogether different course of action. Against all rational considerations of self-interest, he placed her body near a cemetery with blankets readily identifiable as his own, "so she could have a proper buryin'." A "mad-dog" molester and killer of children would have been able to arrange matters more skillfully. A troubled, conflicted, immature, impulsive individual such as Otto, whose affectionate yearnings were clumsy and erratic, and who was unconsciously predetermined to hurt those he loved, would have to leave multiple clues leading to his apprehension. He also would have to commit several stupid, utterly uncharacteristic, and financially unnecessary crimes of breaking and entering his own place of employment and then cashing stolen checks leaving his own identification card, and all this within weeks of a near sexual attack on his stepniece. These acts pointed even more blatantly to the former crime. To Otto, the crime of child molestation was probably greater in its enormity because it temporarily shattered his pride system; the crime of child murder was probably less because it was an attempt to reinstitute the system necessary for his psychic survival.

Like Shakespeare's tragic Moor, Otto, too, "lov'd not wisely but too well."

Some Personal Reflections

I have visited Otto in prison, and we have corresponded for many years while he has served his sentence. His behavior in prison has been exemplary. He began earning college credits through a correspondence course approved by the state. Unfortunately he could not pay his tuition, so he asked me to lend him $120.75 for a few months, which I did. It has been several years since, and though I have never reminded him, the loan is still outstanding.

Sometimes it's the Piper who won't pay.

Postscript

"The Pied Piper of Hamelin" can be seen as a morality tale wherein the townspeople of Hamelin, through their duly elected leaders, tried to have things both ways. They attempted to solve their conflict through chicanery rather than honestly. They wished to have the Pied Piper rid them of their plague of rats while not accepting that the laborer was worthy of his hire. So payment of catastrophic proportions was levied on them. This is the essence of neurotic living as opposed to healthy living: the neurotic sacrifices ultimately worthwhile goals for expedient, anxiety-free devices consisting mostly of pretenses and vanity. This is Horney's Faustian pact. Thus the Pied Piper could epitomize incorruptible reality, which exacts from those who would play fast and loose with their contracts with life the forfeit of their most priceless possession—their hostages to immortality, their children.

Otto also broke his contract with reality. The conflict between two exigent emotional forces was splitting him asunder. His passivity was at war with his repressed aggressiveness, his childlike dependent needs at war with his antisocial machismo behavior, his selfless protector role toward children with his selfish, destructive, lustful using of them. Perhaps metaphorically Robert Browning's Piper symbolized this split into two forces, one for good and the other for evil, by always appearing in a pied cloak.[13] Otto, the black Pied Piper, could not live with his inner hyphen. Reality intruded and swept away his fairy-tale outer garment of fragile defenses. Ultimately, the Piper has to be paid. In this case the price was Eloise's life.

---

13. ". . . the strangest figure!
His queer long coat from heel to head
Was half of yellow and half of red."

Entr'acte VI

Return with your shield or on it!
—Spartan mother

EVERY RED-BLOODED AMERICAN MALE OF MY GENERATION
born between the two world wars should have at least one
war story to impose on some captive audience. This is mine.
   It was the highest level of heroism attained during my
military career. The fact that sheer terror mixed with self-
interested cowardice drove me to such heights should in no
way detract from the valor displayed. It was due primarily to
the lack of basic psycho-pharmacological knowledge and
empathic imagination on the part of certain narrow military
minds in the chain of command that I was not awarded one of
the higher naval decorations. It was the only instance wherein
I single-handedly prevented the murder of a United States
serviceman.
   The time was 1952. The place was the Brooklyn Navy Yard.
I had recently completed a tour of duty as a medical officer

attached to the marine corps in Korea. My overseas duty had been singularly uneventful. The most serious ailment I had treated had been a thrombosed hemorrhoid. In fact I had been considered a good-luck talisman inasmuch as no fatality occurred in my battalion throughout my tour of duty. Upon my return to the United States I had been assigned to the Brooklyn Navy Yard Medical Dispensary—a most peaceful billet preparatory to eventual discharge. Possibilities for military glory were rapidly slipping away.

Then opportunity struck at last. One Saturday night, having pulled the medical watch, I was blissfully sacked out in the room reserved for such purposes. Suddenly I was roused from sleep. That phrase may not adequately capture the true ambience of the occasion. Actually I rose vertically about three feet while remaining rigidly horizontal. Lights flashed on and much commotion and furor swirled about me. When I had settled my wits and body in the more appropriate, gravitationally reasonable position, I found myself confronting a most unusual circumstance. Through a blur I perceived a very tall, very muscular, and very, very, angry marine. He was waving an imposing three-foot length of wood under my nose. He succeeded in attracting my attention. A medical corpsman was fluttering about rather ineffectually in the background protesting that the striking of a ringing blow to the metal frame of a cot was not the method prescribed in the manual for awakening a naval officer. A large hand abruptly juxtaposed to his face sent the corpsman crashing against the wall and considerably diminished the decibel level of my immediate surroundings. My attention remained drawn to the trembling baton. "Get up, Doc, Suh! Get up right now, suh, before Ah kills me a Nigrah!" The ashen face, the forearm blazoned with hash marks, and the master sergeant's stripes brought me into a sudden state of alertness. For a veteran marine noncom, a member of one of the most disciplined services in the world, to deal in such fashion with a commissioned officer spoke more eloquently than words. I grasped the fact that I had before me an individual who could be safely described as being in a state of high dudgeon.

"You'd best get a strong shot of somethin' to put this drunken Nigrah out, Doc, before Ah takes him off. He's beaten up three of mah best men already, and Ah don't aim to be the fourth!" The deep Southern accent struck an ominous note as I hastily dressed. My corpsman grabbed two stretchers as I threw some high-powered barbiturates, needles, and syringes into the emergency kit. As an afterthought and because my good fairy was looking on that evening, I tossed in a bottle of paraldehyde.

For the benefit of the uninitated—and anyone not a chronic alcoholic is uninitiated in this regard—a few words about paraldehyde are in order. Paraldehyde is a drug very similar in chemical structure to formaldehyde. As the latter preserves bodies in a deceased state, so the former preserves alcoholics in a live state, but only barely. Paraldehyde is a clear, colorless, innocent-looking liquid with a smell somewhere between formaldehyde and turpentine and possessing the least desirable aromatic qualities of either. If merely breathed by most mortals it will provoke instant tears. It is guaranteed to knock out a mule, and that most expeditiously. But its one redeeming quality, a quality possessed at that time by no other drug in common usage, was that this evil-smelling, tear-provoking, unmitigatedly obnoxious liquid was tolerated, even loved by an overwhelming majority of alcoholics. It was almost a medical axiom: if you could abide paraldehyde in any shape or form whatsoever, you were an alcoholic. Not any old drunk, mind you, but a bona fide, thoroughly certified, red-eyed, chronic alcoholic.

While speeding through the navy yard in the ambulance, the sergeant blurted out the story. So many colorful but monotonous figures of speech employed by marines under stressful circumstances would have to be deleted in the interests of minimal standards of decency, that it is best I describe the events in more conventional language.

A rather formidable black seaman had developed an abiding dislike of a certain ensign aboard his ship. This ship was now moored at a dock for repairs. The seaman had been on a pass tonight and became roaring drunk with his girl friend. At some point he decided this was the appropriate occasion upon which to make certain anatomical permutations by means of a switchblade on the body of the aforementioned ensign. He deemed this surgical procedure would immensely improve the ensign's disposition, though inevitably discommoding the latter's wife considerably in the years ahead.

Putting his thoughts into immediate operation, he had jumped into his girl friend's car and with her in giggling, giddy attendance roared through the gate of the navy yard. The girl friend had insisted on accompanying him since she had never witnessed this specific surgical procedure, particularly when performed on what she assumed would be a moving target. They proceeded directly to the ship. As luck would have it, the soon-to-be-administered-to ensign happened to be the officer of the deck. The seaman jumped out of the car and dashed up the gangplank. The ensign caught the briefest of glimpses of a flashing switchblade. He instantly divined a purposefulness about the seaman's demeanor with which he was disinclined to cooperate at that time. Some particularly vivid description of a rather radical circumcision about to be performed was transmitted in earthy terms over the night air. This served to galvanize the ensign into certain self-preservative maneuvers. Accordingly he took off at what the navy describes as "flank speed" to parts distant of the ship. The seaman occupied himself totally in hot pursuit in a valiant attempt to engage the enemy.

A certain clamor of voices arose. This produced the desired effect—from the ensign's point of view. By the third rapid circumambulation of the ship, a reassuringly large crowd of seamen had gathered in the rear of this noisy procession. The possessor of the switchblade, upon noticing the imposing numbers of uninvolved naval personnel who seemed intent on interfering with his single-minded purpose, returned whence he had come with considerable alacrity if not utter dispatch. Down the gangplank he leaped and jumped into the aforementioned car to careen off toward the gate.

While these shipboard events had been taking place, the marines guarding the gates of the navy yard had been brooding rather darkly over their previous dereliction of duty in allowing an unauthorized vehicle to penetrate so impudently the hallowed precincts of government property. What went in should eventually come out. They prepared for this eventuality by securely locking all gates.

Thus a scene took place in the guardhouse by the gate which, though not witnessed directly by me, could be readily reconstructed by certain consequences that became quickly evident. Upon entering the room I realized that not a piece of furniture and very few panes of glass were still intact. Lamps, desks, chairs, and other military impedimenta had been overturned or otherwise dealt with severely. An enormous black seaman was seated—sporadically—in the only chair remaining in the upright position. Three marines, all somewhat the worse for wear, were standing over the seaman with clubs clutched in shaking hands. Cuts, abrasions, and multiple swellings on the faces of all participants were noted briefly.

The instigator of my rude awakening joined his men with a display of enthusiasm greater than I would have deemed desirable at that particular moment. The latter spoke. "You bettah give this buck a shot right now, Doc, or Ah'm gonna kill him, so help me God!" The sergeant was beginning to sound like a broken record. The seaman rose drunkenly to his feet, but a sharp rap on the skull put him down again promptly. He seemed essentially unaffected, however, and glared steadily at me. I remember noticing a complete absence of any white showing in his eyes, only red sclera and brown irises—and pinpoint pupils indicating anger, not fear. (I wondered what my pupils were like at that precise moment— fully dilated, I suspected.) Another imminent volcanic eruption was rumbling ominously under the surface.

With trembling fingers I managed to fill a syringe with the most potent barbiturates in the emergency kit and approached my "patient" with the feeble little needle. Few warriors ever entered mortal combat with a smaller sword, or less confidence in their only weapon. "No white _____ officer is gonna kill me with no poison!" spake the seaman. He then described in precise and vivid anatomical terms how he proposed to invade my bodily integrity with the syringe and needle. And the stretcher as well. (I considered that last riposte a rather farfetched idea, but thought better of pointing this out to him.)

"You beat up on my man anymore, and I'll get the NAACP on you." This from the seaman's girl friend jiggling up and down in the corner. That was not exactly what the occasion called for—especially with the southern brethren in attendance. Here I was with extremists to the right of me, extremists to the left of me, and either a drunken crazy man or a crazy drunk in front of me. The situation was pregnant with possibilities—very few of them desirable.

Suddenly the paraldehyde occurred to me. I filled a large two-ounce tumbler to the brim and a one-ounce tumbler halfway. Handing the seaman the large one, in an excess of zeal and a misguided sense of fair play, I proposed, "I'll drink some of this lovely liquid to prove it's not poison if you will also. It'll settle both of our nerves." The seaman appeared minimally reassured. I deemed the auspicious moment was upon us. Suiting action to words, I sipped daintily and tentatively from my tumbler. The scene became transfigured in a most remarkable and instantaneous manner. The back of my throat seemed to burst into flames. I lost all interest in mere earthly concerns, being transfixed by visions of Roman rockets ascending magnificently into a galactic conglomerate of red, blue, and vividly orange stars. Planets veered crazily in their orbits. Spatial relations were transmogrified utterly. Temporal relations were suspended indefinitely and absolutely. As I swayed precariously on some newly attained axis, the seaman, I was subsequently informed, downed his potion neatly. He was then proffered and enthusiastically accepted another tumbler filled by my quick-witted corpsman. The latter had rather smoothly retrieved the bottle as it fell from my hand, which had become fully occupied more essentially. It had clasped my throat in a death grip, probably in a desperate attempt to keep the head from exploding from the neck. I was subsequently informed that one black and one white form in perfect simultaneity became rigid and fell like blocks of ice in opposite directions. Both were caught somewhat short of the floor and instant shattering. The insensate forms were then placed on separate stretchers, one to be deposited in the naval brig and the other in the medical dispensary.

Fortunately no further medical emergencies occurred that night, as the medical officer on duty was hors de combat for a period of twelve hours. During that time all personnel in the

Brooklyn Navy Yard became practicing Christian Scientists whether aware of their temporary conversion or not. And the worst of it all was not a single erstwhile trustworthy corpsman would so much as peep into the room to ascertain if vital signs were still functioning in said medical officer. It seems there is another characteristic of paraldehyde I had failed to mention; a recent recipient exhales an odor for days afterward that reduces strong men to tears and initiates automatic movements to depart the scene with the utmost haste.

As the story made the rounds the next week, certain medical personnel attempted to write me up for a medal for heroism above and beyond the call of duty as well as for a Purple Heart for grievous wounds sustained in the service of my country. I felt it was only simple justice. After all, I had surpassed in valor even those glorious Spartan warriors of yore; I had returned from battle not only with my shield but on it.

Lazarus

And would it have been worth it, after all,
. . . .
To have squeezed the universe into a ball
To roll it towards some overwhelming question,
To say: "I am Lazarus come from the dead,
Come back to tell you all, I shall tell you all" —
If one, settling a pillow by her head,
Should say: "That is not what I meant at all.
That is not it, at all."
—T.S. Eliot

I offer my apologies to those readers who may take offense at a biblical story's being grouped with fairy tales. No disrespect toward religion is intended. The story of Lazarus is used here merely to illustrate one murderer's delusional appropriation of the story; it was *his* fairy tale.

Alice Brickw

O THEN THIS GUY COMES INTO THE BAR, WHAT'S-HIS-name, the guy what [sic] got killed?" Inasmuch as Dan was on trial for felony murder, this cavalier indifference to his victim's identify was particularly striking. Somehow it would seem that after taking another human being's life, one should at least recall his name.

Dan readily described meeting Harry, a casual acquaintance, in a tavern. Harry suggested they pick up a few dollars by robbing the store of a reputed homosexual named Gus. They arranged to meet Gus in another tavern, whence the three repaired to Gus's store. At a prearranged signal, Dan grabbed Gus around the neck while Harry pounded him in the face with his fists. In Dan's word. "He wouldn't go down. Harry handed me a pipe. I hit him on the head. He went down but still wasn't knocked out. So Harry told me to put the pipe across his neck, and we both stood on the ends of the pipe. I pried it loose finally and told Harry not to kill him. Harry said he had to kill him because Gus knew his identity. I said, 'No, let's just rob the store.' So I went looking for money. I had to go back several times to stop Harry, who kept stomping on Gus's neck or kicking him. Then I felt Gus's pulse and said, 'He's dead.' Harry said he wasn't. We left. Outside Harry said he *was* dead. I said, 'If he's dead, he's dead. Can't bring him back.' " Dan's last comment did not seem particularly significant, although it was duly noted.

Two days after this felony homicide, Dan was involved in a meaningless altercation in a nearby bar in which he drew a knife against several opponents. He was arrested but released on bail. To bring oneself to the attention of the police shortly after a well-publicized homicide in the immediate vicinity does not demonstrate the highest level of self-interest or self-preservation.

Several days later Harry was picked up and questioned by the police about Gus's murder. Harry had been observed leaving the tavern with Gus shortly before the murder. He accused Dan of planning and carrying out the entire operation, with himself as an unwilling witness. Dan was arrested and readily confessed to participating in the crime in concert with Harry. They both signed confessions describing their differing versions of their respective participation in the crime. An ultimate confrontation between the two in the legal arena seemed inevitable.

Dan's past history revealed familial neglect, indifference, poverty, and degradation to a marked degree. His Irish-American parents argued and fought constantly. Dan was the eleventh of twelve children born of this mismatch. Several of his siblings had been in reformatories and prisons for a variety of minor offenses such as truancy, waywardness, and so on. His mother had been diagnosed as a probable schizophrenic of low normal intelligence. His father, a day laborer, was an alcoholic who deserted the family when Dan was three. He did not support his family but would return sporadically to demand sexual favors, frequently in the presence of the children. He died four years prior to Dan's present legal difficulty.

Dan represented a lifelong "stormy personality" (to use Silvano Arieti's term from *The Interpretation of Schizophrenia*). At eight years of age he had threatened a nun in school with a knife. He once fired three times at one of his brothers with a 22-caliber rifle but fortunately missed. He was perennially truant, a wayward child, guilty of many petty crimes, and flew into uncontrollable rages upon minimal provocation. He had spent most of the years from fourteen to his present twenty-three years of age in and out of prisons (with several escapes), and mental hospitals. Seven years before the homicide, state-hospital psychiatrists diagnosed him as a paranoid schizophrenic with a history of suicidal attempts, auditory hallucinations, and delusions of alien influence. He had attempted suicide on three occasions by swallowing nails and open safety pins. Two years ago one state-hospital psychiatrist quoted Dan as saying, "I'm glad you caught me because I felt I wanted to murder somebody." In his last hospitalization, lasting more than four months, he had received a long course of electroshock therapy and tranquilizers. Shortly before discharge from this hospital he begged one psychiatrist individually and the medical staff· generally to send him home only on weekend passes rather than discharge him outright because he was terrified of his lack of control over his hostile impulses. The medical staff, pleading a shortage of beds, refused. He was propelled back on the streets seven weeks before the murder.

On the rare occasions in the preceding decade when Dan had been at liberty he had worked sporadically at menial jobs, burglarized occasionally, been a procurer for homosexual and heterosexual prostitutes as well as a male prostitute himself, lived in common-law marriages with several prostitutes, and been involved in frequent impulsive assaults, usually using a knife.

In the midst of this seemingly unrelieved antisocial behavior, there was a curiously tender streak toward children, stray dogs, and the downtrodden, particularly prostitutes. He had befriended several prostitutes, buying them clothes and food without ever seeking favors in return. He felt at ease with members of these three groups and trusted them as he had never been able to trust those belonging to the mass of society.

The key to the determination of Dan's mental state, after a lengthy series of psychiatric examinations, finally rested on whether or not he had in fact been experiencing auditory and visual hallucinations. These hallucinations supported and helped maintain a vast, all-encompassing delusional system which long antedated the crime for which he was being tried. When Dan was fifteen his brother, who had been killed in World War II, appeared to him while he was awake. Though this apparition appeared only infrequently, it usually warned him of impending danger. It also attempted to compel him to kill his common-law wife and commit other acts of violence. Ten years before the crime he attended lectures of a quasi-religious group which preached reincarnation. Though he did not believe in it at the time, six years later he decided it was probably true because he then started hearing a voice he was convinced was God's. This voice assured him of the validity of reincarnation. He thus incorporated this quasi-religion into his already developing delusional system. Four years ago after his father's death, the father joined the dead brother as a double apparition. These two figures appeared more and more frequently over the years and beckoned to him but no longer spoke.

There now occurred a split in his hallucinations, in which only God's voice spoke while the brother and father continued to appear but remained silent. God's voice began to direct his major actions increasingly. He would be told to rob this or that place and was assured by God that he had every right to the riches of others merely because he desired them. This bond with God remained mutually advantageous except at those times when Dan felt God became too brutal, particularly when He commanded Dan to throw acid in the faces of some children and prostitutes he had befriended. (It should be noted that Dan had severe pitting of the face due to adolescent acne.) Fortunately, he would argue successfully with God in these instances, though the struggle would invariably prove exhausting.

Finally God revealed that Dan would die and then return to earth in his own form or another's, whichever he preferred. Dan firmly chose his own form because he then felt he would be the first individual universally recognized as returning from the dead. This would prove that his God was more powerful than anyone else's. He would then, after returning to earth, preach to everyone and convert followers who would proceed to kill all nonbelievers. Harry, his accomplice and accuser, had a special fate reserved for him. He would be blinded and completely paralyzed by strategic severing of muscle tendons so that he would have to lie forever immobile and helpless, listening only for Dan's footsteps. Dan felt a public electrocution for murder would be far more convincing proof to the world than the biblical story of Lazarus that his relationship to God was unique and special over all others. Upon returning from the dead he would convert the entire world and set it all "straight." He dismissed with lordly disdain any questions about the details of his precise program for accomplishing this not-altogether-modest task. He stated he would have to die first to be informed of the specifics by God. After Dan's work had been completed, God would spirit his father, brother, and himself off to another planet where he would relax and enjoy himself with children throughout eternity. His delusional system was complete and airtight.

Having been brought into the case as a psychiatrist for the defense, I reported my findings to Dan's attorneys. It was an open-and-shut case. The other defense psychiatrist and the two state-appointed psychiatrists had submitted reports agreeing that Dan was suffering from chronic paranoid schizophrenia of over ten years duration. The illness or reaction type had progressed inexorably to a probably irreversible stage. He was a present and future menace of the highest order to society and should be hospitalized forthwith for an indefinite period in a state mental hospital for the criminally insane. All seemed in order. Unanimity reigned supreme. The dreaded and often dreadful "battle of the experts" would be avoided. The wheels of justice should roll smoothly and swiftly.

It is at moments like this that one is apt to forget the inevitability of Murphy's law: "Anything that can possibly go wrong, will."

A series of ironies and misfortunes plagued the medico-legal outcome of this case. As described earlier Dan had literally begged the psychiatric staff of the state hospital not to

discharge him because he doubted his control of his hostile
impulses. In spite of a record of psychotic delusions and
hallucinations compelling him to commit antisocial and
violent acts, a history of frequent escapes from hospitals and
prisons, and a poor hospital adjustment, Dan had been discharged seven weeks before the murder.

Secondly, Dan *wanted* to be found guilty by the court. His
voices from God mandated that he be electrocuted in the first
stage of his Lazarus reenactment prior to his conversion of the
whole world.

Thirdly, the defense attorneys were responsible and ethical
persons who felt a clear obligation to protect society from an
extremely disturbed individual who had killed once and was
likely to kill again in response to his hallucinatory commands.
The defense psychiatrists, because of their position as agents
for Dan's attorneys, elicited even more information from Dan
than the state psychiatrists, since Dan was more relaxed with
them. They were more convinced than anyone else in the case
that Dan was truly a menace. The jury had been selected and
the trial was about to begin. Then the defense attorneys in a
conference with their psychiatrists just before the trial
casually brought up the matter of the voluntary nature of
Dan's confession. Both defense psychiatrists raised doubts
that they could testify in all good conscience that Dan was of
such sound mind and free will as to be able to sign a valid
confession. All at once the fat was in the fire. To the dismay
and chagrin of everyone on the defense side, it occurred to us
for the first time that the state investigators either had not
done their homework or had been unable to produce
corroborating evidence of Dan's confession. No confession—
no case. Dan could walk out of that courtroom a free man. And
we all were going to be the reluctant accomplices to a legal
nightmare.

The legal momentum kept pushing us on a dangerous
course. The defense psychiatrists established a preponderance
of evidence attesting to the seriousness of Dan's mental
illness. A four-inch-thick summary of state mental hospital
records was placed before the court. Forty separate
psychiatrists over the past decade had written comments
indicating that Dan was dangerous and psychotic. These

records long antedated the present crime and spoke categorically against any implications of malingering. Our recent examinations had merely confirmed the validity of these previous observations.

The thorny issue was whether an individual who had broken with reality and followed imaginary commands from a personage he identified as God could be considered competent to sign a confession of his own "free will." To many psychiatrists this is a logical absurdity. Dan's passivity and suggestibility were emphasized. Even the fact that he wanted to be found guilty and electrocuted to fulfill his delusional messianic vision could be seen as raising the possibility that he would confess to any crime he was accused of, whether actually guilty or not. Dan had told a detective, "I would have signed anything, even killing Kennedy, because of the way I felt in my head." (We did not believe the confession was false but had to testify to the theoretical possibility. It is important to bear in mind the defense *has* to bring out these legal points or the outcome of the trial could be reversed on appeal.)

I raised another point. In the voluminous state hospitals' records, a single odd sheet of paper called attention to itself. It sat there ticking away like a time bomb and had to be defused. The clinical director of one hospital stated that Dan was a psychopath without psychosis and a chronic liar and malingerer. This note opposed the majority opinion of his own medical staff, and was remarkable in that it was written six weeks *after* Dan had escaped from this hospital after knocking an attendant unconscious and threatening a nurse with a knife and a broken bottle. Also it was written in the presence of the sheriff of Dan's home county, who was obviously being encouraged by the clinical director to double his efforts to recapture Dan, who was then at large. The physician stated categorically he felt Dan lied about his voices in order to be transferred from prison to state hospitals, where he could effect escape more easily. (Having spent most of his life in institutions, Dan was a talented escape artist by this time, though he usually reappeared at the hospitals after brief drunken sprees and begged to be readmitted.) He closed his note by strongly recommending that Dan not be returned to his hospital but admitted to another hospital in that state with far tighter security provisions. In fact, this was what happened when Dan was apprehended. It was from the more secure hospital that Dan had been discharged just before the murder.

I had to address myself to this note. Ironically the clinical director was a close personal friend and neighbor. I held him in the highest professional esteem and so stated on the witness stand. Without having talked to him about this matter (considering it probably unethical during a court proceeding), I deduced that the note in the hospital chart was of a purely administrative nature—especially since it was written in the presence of a law-enforcement official six weeks after Dan had escaped from the hospital, and ran counter to the opinion of the entire medical staff in all their previous evaluations. I speculated that the clinical director was rightfully concerned about the future physical safety of his attendants and nurses and felt Dan should be handled in a facility better equipped for dangerous patients. Finally it should be mentioned that clinical directors, since they have overall responsibility for thousands of patients, rarely see any given patient for more than ten minutes at a staff meeting.

The judge adjourned the session after receiving testimony similar to mine from the other defense psychiatrist. The two state psychiatrists agreed with our diagnosis but felt Dan was capable of signing a valid confession.

A long weekend was ahead for the judge. The sympathy of both the prosecution and the defense was with him. He emerged several days later with a scholarly legal decision admitting Dan's confession into evidence. The lengthy decision was thorough, logical, and legally brilliant. From a psychiatric point of view it was pure jabberwocky. The judge fundamentally insisted on a logical explanation for each significant action and verbalization of Dan's illogical and insane mind. Otherwise Dan had to be a liar and a malingerer. He took a prodigious swipe at my comments about the clinical director's administrative note. He denied the validity of my explanation and gave far greater credence to four months of personal and staff observation of Dan in the hospital as opposed to a mere six hours of examination by two defense psychiatrists. He concluded Dan was perhaps mentally ill but was definitely a liar who feigned his hallucinations for opportunistic reasons in order to be transferred from prison to hospitals so that he could escape more easily.

The judge then called the defense and prosecuting attorneys to the bench. He informed the defense attorney that he strongly urged him to plead his client guilty of second-degree murder and the prosecuting attorney to accept the plea forthwith. He told them in a quietly firm manner that he wanted the case disposed of within the hour. Both attorneys recognized the implicit meaning behind the judge's words. It was so disposed. A sigh of relief was breathed by all concerned.

Dan was sentenced to the state prison for life as legally sane. The warden and guards at that prison took one long look at Dan, whom they knew well from former times, and promptly transferred him to the ward for the criminally insane in the nearest state hospital, where he resides to this day. I regularly receive Christmas cards at Easter time from Dan with cryptic messages such as, "You'll know what was meant by this card."

After the trial I got in touch with my friend of the troublesome note. I asked him if he remembered Dan. He most assuredly did and remembered writing the note. When asked how long he had personally examined Dan, he expostulated, "I never laid eyes on him in my life! You know it's a physical impossibility for a clinical director to examine most patients in a three-thousand-bed hospital. I wrote that note in front of a county sheriff so that the police would get hopping and apprehend Dan. He was a dangerous paranoid schizophrenic, as any psychiatrically knowledgeable person would know who read the hospital records. All one has to do is weigh a chart like his to know. I just didn't want him returned to my hospital, as he had terrorized my staff in his escape attempts. Any number of nurses threatened to resign if he were ever readmitted. I'm trying to run a hospital, not a goddamn prison!" When informed of the legal significance his note had assumed, he was positively apoplectic. He was indignant that the judge had not telephoned him to clear up such a potentially disastrous misunderstanding. Conceivably if a trial had actually taken place, Dan could have been electrocuted as a sane criminal on the basis of a note signed by a psychiatrist who had never actually examined him.

A final turn of the screw. Dan was the chief witness for the state in the subsequent murder trial of Harry. Dan reenacted the murder before another jury, complete with standing on the pipe and further details. With four psychiatrists and four inches of hospital records, Dan had been declared legally sane in his own trial. With no psychiatric testimony but merely a hint here and an innuendo there, Harry's attorney was able to convince that jury that Dan was much too insane to be a reliable witness in Harry's trail. It was a brilliant courtroom demonstration of the "soft sell." By being allowed to form their own conclusions, the jurors probably felt most psychologically astute. Harry walked out of the courtroom a free man.

Dan requested another interview with me. He sadly commented that his God had had the last word after all. Because Dan had temporarily lost faith in Him and allowed his attorney to plead him guilty to second-degree murder instead of allowing him to be electrocuted, Harry had been set free. Dan remembered " 'Vengeance is mine; I will repay,' saith the Lord." Henceforth he would trust his voices and not the vagaries of man-made legalities. His God would ultimately set things right.

As we were parting for the last time, Dan broke down in tears. It was the only time I ever saw him reveal any strong feelings. He stated that he had admired and trusted both the defense psychiatrists. During the trial, though, we had both testified that his voices were products of his own imagination and did not emanate from God. He wondered if he really was mentally ill because he heard voices which did not sound like his own. He expressed some doubt as to whether his voices were from God but considerable doubt as to whether he would be punished because he had broken faith with Him. His ambivalence was naked and awesome. I comforted him as best I could.

And So to Court

The legal ramifications and outcome have already been recounted. I would add only this warning to psychiatrists and psychologists who may consider testifying in court: be prepared for the unexpected. A case that appears clear-cut and routine from a purely scientific point of view may take novel twists in a legal framework. A certain good-natured equanimity about the vagaries of fortune and the unpredictability of events has to be cultivated. Attorneys-at-law eventually reconcile themselves to the harsh reality that perfect justice is not always accomplished because it is perforce dispensed by fallible and limited human intelligences within a framework of legal conventions and rules. These rules represent the product of centuries of effort by brilliant legal minds in attempts to build into the system basic fairness for the accused and accuser alike. One should not have to be reminded that perfection is not to be expected this side of the gates of paradise.

There is one truth I believe. As Horace Walpole said: "The whole world is a comedy to those that think, a tragedy to those that feel." In a courtroom life is often presented in its starkest forms. Persons of good will have to reconcile themselves to the hyphen of life's comedy-tragedy or they will abandon the law and the courtroom to more cynical minds.

The Illness

Dan was a chronic schizophrenic of the paranoid type. His paranoid system of thinking, like Robin's, was encapsulating, closed, and immutable. He had escaped into a fantasied world where inner thoughts had been projected outward into hallucinatory constructs of a supernatural potency. Against such grandiose convictions the impact of human intervention is feeble indeed. Delusions such as Dan's, which have been fixed for many years, are seldom if ever abandoned. To disrupt or loosen such a system of thinking would uncover frightening depths of despair and worthlessness and plunge Dan into a devastating depression—a depression he had unconsciously fled by formulating his bizarre ideas in the first place. A person possessed of such a fragile sense of self-worth gives up such fantasied glorification most reluctantly (many authorities think never).

There is one rare, fortuitous outcome of this form of schizophrenia. Just as some cancers are so virulent and fast-growing that the tumor cells actually outgrow their own blood supply and die off spontaneously, allowing the host-body to survive, so, too, some chronic paranoid schizophrenics "bleach out" over the course of many years. They improve by regression. The pathological ideas remain, but the individual has regressed to such a level of apathy that he no longer can mobilize or focus sufficient mental energies to respond to the ideas. He becomes less of a real person but relatively harmless from the community's vantage point. He withdraws from most interpersonal contacts, restricts his living to the irreducible minimum, and exists on an automaton-like level. Such individuals can be released under outside supervision after decades of hospitalization with little or no risk. Schizophrenics can present bland exteriors; inside they thrash about unmercifully. Eventually in some, the fires burn low. Society may then, to some extent, reclaim the burned-out husks.

Why Did It Happen?

Seen from the vantage point of Dan's messianic delusional system, the murder of "What's-his-name" was truly incidental. Dan's God-given right to possess the worldly riches of others took precedence over any consideration of another's mere right to live. However, Dan's remark after the homicide, "If he's dead, he's dead. Can't bring him back," takes on a new significance. His nonchalance toward another's life represents, in his distorted frame of reference, not arrogance but the inevitable condescension of an immortal toward the merely human.

Psychodynamically, Dan seemed to have been a terrified younger child in the family, brutalized by his father and bullied by other siblings. He had sudden and unpredictable outbursts of uncontrolled aggressiveness with minimal provocation. In his subsequent antisocial escapades in prisons and mental hospitals, he was rarely the instigator but more often the suggestible dupe of more forceful accomplices. Gradually he regressed from sociopathic behavior to a schizophrenic level where his self-effacing trends were in the foreground and his expansive trends were externalized into a delusional covenant with God. Hallucinatory confirmation of this special relationship cemented the supernatural bond. A passive acceptance of God's commands (except for the exhausting struggles when He appeared too vindictive) entitled Dan to the fringe benefits of unrestricted access to the possessions of others. While he asserted this neurotic claim by rolling and robbing Gus, his accomplice opted for homicide to prevent identification. Dan, delusionally enveloped in his divine mission, felt no such precautions were necessary. After assisting in the initial aggravated assault on Gus, he was easily distracted by the search for booty and made only half-hearted attempts to prevent his accomplice from completing the act.

It appears likely that the peak of tension and conflict between Dan's self-effacing passivity and his sporadic aggressiveness occurred during the initial assault on Gus. This assault permitted the assertion of his inalienable right to rob. During Dan's return to his former psychic safety zone of passivity, Gus's life was forfeited. As shown by Dan's indifference to his victim's name, the murder was only incidental. What was exigent was carrying out God's command to rob and then returning to his status quo—his less anxious resting state.

Some Personal Reflections

Dan, a chronic paranoid schizophrenic, is a classic example of the unholy trinity: the Bible in the left hand, a lethal weapon in the right, and the paranoid schizophrenic in the middle. It is the most potentially dangerous mixture among the mentally ill.

Two recent well-publicized cases represent similar examples of this unholy trinity: Charles Manson of the Tate-LaBianca murders and David Berkowitz, the suspected 44-caliber killer. Although I am violating one of the cardinal principles of psychiatry—never to diagnose an individual one has not personally examined—I cannot resist pointing out certain similarities. Manson, the self-styled "Son of Man," felt he received supernatural messages—often through Beatles records which he related to biblical passages—was invulnerable to death, and had a divine mission to redress the iniquities of the world after a racially inspired war of extermination. Berkowitz, the self-confessed "Son of Sam," received messages from a six-thousand-year-old man through a dog, perceived divine "signs" commanding him to kill at specific times and places, and was planning a *Götterdämmerung*-like mass killing when captured. Manson refused to present an insanity defense, so he was never officially diagnosed a paranoid schizophrenic. At the time of writing, Berkowitz has not been tried and therefore his diagnosis is also not official. However, I feel that the preponderance of information that has appeared in newspapers and books makes the diagnosis of paranoid schizophrenia quite likely in both cases.

Many lay people have the mistaken notion that a legal determination of "innocent by reason of insanity" is a miscarriage of justice and a "cop-out." They also feel such disposition of a case offers society far less protection against further murders by a mentally ill person than a lengthy prison sentence. That is not necessarily so. It is well to bear in mind that Manson is soon coming up for parole after serving the minimal period of his sentence.

Inasmuch as there are fifty states, with many variations in their statutes, I can state the following only in general terms. After an individual has been declared legally insane, he or she is usually remanded to a state hospital for the criminally insane. In very few states would such facilities be easily confused with country clubs. If the medical staff is at all competent, a chronic paranoid schizophrenic is recognized as being exceedingly dangerous, rarely cured, and strongly recidivistic. Considerable caution is usually exercised before such a person is ever recommended for release. In many states the individual has to appear before a judge, who also has to approve his release, thus providing society with two-fold protection—a medical screening and a legal review. And there is a little-recognized third protection—the illness itself. A marked number of chronic paranoid schizophrenics regress or deteriorate in personality organization over the years to the point where even the most unsophisticated psychiatrist could not overlook the extent of the disability. It is far more likely that prison officials rather than hospital authorities would commit egregious errors in their evaluation of the final stages of schizophrenic deterioration. Furthermore the progressive withdrawal of the chronic schizophrenic and his lack of interest in any but the most superficial and transient interpersonal exchanges renders him far less dangerous to his fellow beings.

Finally, in the opinion of most observers, paranoid schizophrenics suffer far more from their never-ending internal agonies, from the sense of utter isolation, from the ferocious racking by their opposing emotions, and from the unbearable panic states they undergo than from any punishment ever devised or meted out by a humane society. Many such victims experience years of an existence as close to a life in hell as any that medieval Florentine genius ever imagined.

With most chronic paranoid schizophrenics, especially those who have killed, John Greenleaf Whittier's words from "Skipper Ireson's Ride" most accurately describe their anguish:

What is the shame that clothes the skin
To the nameless horror that lives within?
. . . .
Hate me and curse me, — I only dread
The hand of God and the face of the dead!

Entr'acte VII

I simply want to tell you that there are
some men in this world who were born to do our
unpleasant jobs for us.
—Harper Lee

THIS ANECDOTE IS NOT AN AMUSING ONE. IT INVOLVES A psychiatrist with whom I had worked on several murder cases. He was a highly respected physician, always willing to assist colleagues or law-enforcement officials in intricate situations. This was not his native land, but he possessed that strong sense of community responsibility that distinguishes the truly civilized man. He was an accomplished musician, a man of vast culture, and a gentleman in the true sense of the word. Perhaps it was his gentleness that was at the root of it all.

Unlike many of us, he took on the unpleasant, the dangerous cases. My friend had treated a certain patient on and off for many years. The patient would never continue therapy on a regular basis but appeared only when in acute

171

distress. On several occasions the psychiatrist had had him hospitalized on a voluntary basis as deeply disturbed. He knew his patient could be dangerous at certain stages of his illness. At one such time, he informed the patient and the patient's wife that immediate hospitalization was imperative. The patient was not enthusiastic but tentatively agreed to cooperate. The wife became obdurate, however, She refused her consent and minimized the extent of the pathology. This is a common reaction of many relatives of the mentally disturbed during the initial illness. But after several previously successful hospitalizations, it was particularly unreasonable in this instance. My friend pleaded, cajoled, and recommended in the firmest terms—all to no avail. Without his wife's approval the patient would not consent to be hospitalized voluntarily.

The psychiatrist could have done what many of us do under similar circumstances and discharged the patient from his care since his professional advice was not being followed. Being the kind of person he was, my friend decided to temporize and treat the patient as best he could in his office. The patient was a suffering human being, and the community had to be safeguarded, even if imperfectly. My friend saw nobody else assuming responsibility. So he delayed and delayed, always playing for the time that the wife would modify her position.

And then time ran out.

One day the patient appeared for his appointment, loud shouts were heard, and then a single shot from a pistol. The psychiatrist was killed instantly. The patient was promptly sent to a hospital for the criminally insane.

Does it signify? As with any profound movement in the affairs of men, what improves the lot of many invariably causes misfortune to the few. The pendulum has swung at this time toward assiduous safeguarding of the civil rights of the mentally ill. When reputable psychotherapists, however, are handcuffed by overly strict man-made laws rather than being able to rely on their scientific, clinical judgment within broad outlines of constitutional protections, people can be injured. Sometimes it's the person trying to help.

I wonder if the relatives or the promulgators of laws ever consider deeply some of these consequences? Or do they pass them off as the error of the therapist, who after all is supposed to possess the knowledge to appreciate the hazards of his or her profession?

Errors of the heart—as well as those of the head—can kill.

Madame Butterfly

[Last night I dreamt I was a butterfly.]
I do not know whether I was then a
man dreaming I was a
butterfly, or whether I am
now a butterfly dreaming
I am a man.
—Chuang Tzu

A ND WITH THAT THE DREAM AND THE NOTHINGNESS vanished. Everything was suddenly real. It was so real. And I fired. I kept on firing and firing.!"

As I listened to Rose I thought how different her story was from that of most criminals, who maintain they woke up with the smoking gun in hand and no memory of committing a murder. She woke up from a dream and *then* fired. And fired and fired.

When the jail matron had led her into the interview room for our first meeting, Rose clung to her as if she were her mother. When we were alone, Rose couldn't sit in a chair for more than a minute at a time. She fluttered about the room, now picking up an object on the desk and examining it listlessly, now looking bewilderingly and fleetingly at me, now

177

perching on the edge of the desk. She rested for a moment and then wandered off again. She resembled nothing so much as a trapped butterfly flitting here and there, never deciding where finally to settle.

We made contact. She didn't shake hands as much as rest a moist limb in my hand for the briefest of moments. Her hair was tangled and unkempt. The jail smock hung listlessly on her emaciated frame. She was all angles. And frightened—she looked frightened to death. Bit by bit, in spite of her obvious confusion and agitation, her story unfolded.

Rose was the fifth of eleven children of a couple of Italian extraction. After an uneventful childhood and youth, she graduated from high school and soon thereafter married. This union lasted less than a year because of brutalities she suffered at the hands of her husband as well as certain sexual indignities he inflicted on her. After the divorce she married John and now seven years later was twenty-eight years of age and the mother of a boy of three and a girl one year old. In the past two weeks she had been widowed—as a direct consequence of her having fired five bullets from a 38-caliber pistol into her husband's body while he lay on the living-room sofa.

At the time of their marriage Rose was aware John drank heavily. It was an article of faith to her, however, that the love of a good woman would shortly overcome this idiosyncrasy. And so it turned out; John worked hard in an automobile agency, and they set up housekeeping. He moonlighted by purchasing a small store selling automobile accessories. Soon he became dissatisfied with working for somebody else, quit his salaried position, and tried to support his family solely on the profits from the store. The move was premature, competition was stiffer than anticipated, and the business began operating at a loss. Debts piled up. John's drinking began again and became progressively worse. When creditors telephoned or wrote dunning letters, John would force Rose to deal with them while he adjourned to his favorite tavern. To a meek, self-effacing person like Rose, having to stand up to angry creditors was an abomination of the first order. John lost one part-time job after another, neglected his business for weeks at a time, and drank continuously. His pattern evolved into week-long alcoholic bouts during which he would stay away from home, sleep in parked cars behind taverns, and return to Rose at odd hours in a pitiful condition. In the winter months he contracted pneumonia on two occasions as a result of exposure at night while semicomatose. Finally he skidded to the lowest level of the alcoholic hierarchy: the wino. When he was totally without money, Rose felt the drinking would perforce stop. In this she was sadly mistaken. She was ignorant of the ubiquitous banking system among alcoholics: that well-entrenched custom whereby the wino flush with money sets up drinks for the rest, not out of generosity so much as to store up notes payable on demand when his own funds have been dissipated. John's credit rating was of the highest order and he was able to continue drinking for six to nine months without recourse to panhandling. At one point John had been out of work for a year without attempting seriously to obtain another position. Rose had returned to her old job and worked until the seventh month of her first pregnancy. Now, being tied down with two toddlers, such a solution was out of the question; John's drinking made him unreliable, even as a baby-sitter for his own children.

Rose complained principally of an absence of any semblance of communication with her husband. He would impulsively purchase major items such as an automobile or a sofa without discussing it with her, plunging them ever deeper into debt. If Rose remonstrated, he would promise never to repeat that particular offense or stalk out of the house indignantly and become intoxicated. But, as Rose said, "I never hated my husband. He had a lot of good in him except for the drinking. I always tried not to argue with him so he wouldn't lose his temper. Frequently he would strike me if I questioned his actions. Only twice in my life did I ever use profanity when he came home filthy and drunk. Both times he grabbed me, pulled my head back by the hair until I thought my neck would snap, forced me on my knees, and made me say I was sorry."

This absence of any true awareness of hatred toward John was quite striking. His rudeness, arrogance, stubbornness, and unreliability estranged most of their friends and relatives, leaving Rose more and more cut off. She had always enjoyed the company of intimate groups of people, but this was to be no more. Whenever Rose would become fed up and resolve to leave him, John would beg her to stay in the most heartrending manner and threaten to kill himself. His desperate need, adroitly interspersed with that magic word "love," was the open sesame to her heart time after time. Besides, her foremost concern was always the babies, and when sober, John was a devoted father. He loved to frolic with the children and buy them candy and toys. It was surely only the drinking which made him impatient and irascible with them. His lack of responsibility in money matters had no connection with his deep and abiding love for his babies. Or did it? He waxed so eloquent and beat his breast so sincerely when the remorse was on him during the hangover stage that he would melt a heart of stone. So Rose forgot and forgave.

In the week preceding the crime, there occurred a concatenation of events which was to stir up more intense regret and guilt among a greater number of people than I have ever observed before or since. After the newspapers' clarion call rang out, "Wife Murders Sleeping Husband," several of the most well-intentioned members of Rose's community spent sleepless nights agonizing, "Was I the one who failed her?" "Should I have guessed that. . ." "Could I have surmised that . . ." "Why did I wait until. . ." And would you or I have done more?

It began when John was offered back his former job at two hundred and twenty-five dollars a week. The family was living from hand to mouth, yet John arrogantly insisted upon a dramatic increase in his previous salary. He was not rehired and Rose became frantic.

Being a devout Roman Catholic, she turned to her parish priest. He was initially attentive, then grew incensed as the tale unfolded, and finally was so outraged by the years of abuse and degradation she had tolerated that he advised her to leave John immediately. She returned home more depressed than ever. She had been too ashamed to tell the priest that it was her second marriage, as she feared he might have castigated her for "living in sin" in the eyes of the church.

She called her mother-in-law. That worthy had long since given up on her prodigal son. She advised Rose to start having affairs with other men, arouse John's jealousy, and that would snap him out of his foolishness. Rose hadn't so much as looked at another man in years, she didn't have a decent dress to her name, and she wouldn't have known the first thing about inaugurating such a program. She was affronted and felt her mother-in-law had the morals of an alley cat.

She next consulted her family physician. He prescribed tranquilizers for her and a psychiatrist for John. She prevailed on John to see the psychiatrist. In a fit of remorse he made an appointment for the next day but at the last moment failed to keep it. The family physician had made an honest but all-too-common error of equating the relative degree of emotional illness of John and Rose with who was most blameworthy. Though John was erring, Rose was sicker. Rose, however, had neglected to reveal to her physician that two days previously she had turned on all the gas jets in the kitchen, waited for a matter of minutes, thought better of causing the death of her sleeping children as well as herself, and turned them off. "I'd look at the babies and think awful things. But I didn't want to harm them. I'd have to run out of the room at those times."

She turned to her two older brothers. They repeated their perennial advice: John was unsalvageable—so leave him. This course seemed unfeasible since she had to maintain a roof over her babies' heads at all cost, and the house was in her name. Also her brothers were unable to assist her financially.

Finally, she tentatively telephoned an attorney regarding possible divorce proceedings. His calendar was so crowded that the first appointment he could give her was one week after the fateful day. And, besides, divorce is expensive.

On the eve of the crime John lurched into the house at 1 A.M. He had been drinking for three days and was in an ugly mood. He flung her off the sofa, where she had been watching television, twisting her arm painfully in the process. He flopped on the sofa wrapped in a cloud of obscenities. She looked up at him from the floor for a long, long moment and felt, "I've had it!" For the first time in all the years of humiliation and tantalizing hopes repeatedly dashed into despair, she asserted herself, and telephoned the police. Thirty minutes later two police officers arrived to find John sleeping peacefully. He was aroused, appeared confused at all the fuss, and became righteously indignant at the unwarranted intrusion on the sanctity of a man's home. The officers listened to Rose's complaints but decided John was cooperative now and could not be arrested unless she swore out a complaint. She wavered for some time but couldn't bring herself to press charges. John spoke so eloquently; it had been only a minor family spat. The police officers debated between themselves. They told Rose to call the station in the morning if she decided to press charges. The police left. John promptly fell asleep. She was utterly alone.

Rose retired for the night. She was surprised that sleep came easily to her that night. It was as if some momentous thing had been settled in her mind, though later she couldn't recall what it was. Early the next morning the children awakened her. She brought them downstairs and fed them breakfast. The children played as usual on the kitchen floor with the pots and pans they pulled out of the cabinets. Rose felt an inner agitation and tremulousness. She paced up and down the room, chain smoking, sipping her coffee, and biting the tips of her fingers. Then she sat at the table and "it" happened.

"I suddenly felt a complete emptiness. I never had that feeling before. I can't explain it. It was like the time I fainted in the hospital years ago, and when I woke up I couldn't remember anything for a few minutes. But this was longer and much worse. I wasn't able to bring myself out of it. I didn't understand it. I still don't remember too clearly. I'm sure I hugged one of the babies. I don't know why I did that. I felt dazed. Then I didn't seem to know where the babies were, and I always know where they are every minute. But everything was so quiet. Usually the children jabber or rattle the pots and pans, but all about me was a nothingness. I couldn't seem to move my head to look for them. All I seemed able to do was to listen for something. Then I was talking on the phone to my girl friend, Pearl. I don't know if I called her or she called me. I don't even remember the phone ringing. But I was talking. Pearl said something about us bowling the next day. Then the call was over. I was trying to think. There was this strange feeling inside me. But everything was quiet. There didn't seem to be anything or anyone else in the world except me. Why didn't I hear the children or the canary or something? It was a nothingness. I don't know how long I sat there. It wasn't terrifying exactly, just a blank. I felt numb, like a stupor I guess, where you don't know what's going on and can't do anything about it anyway. Like a bad dream where you're trying to run, but your feet keep getting bogged down in some sticky muck. It just seemed to be happening to me.

"I stood up and went to the bureau in the living room. The babies' diapers are kept there. As I was rummaging in the drawer, I saw John's gun lying there. I picked it up and was staring at it. I don't know what I was thinking about. I just kept staring and staring at the gun in my hand. John was still lying on the sofa. Suddenly he woke up, saw me with the gun and shouted, 'Stop fooling around there!' And with that the dream and the nothingness vanished. Everything was suddenly real. *It was so real.* And I fired. I kept on firing. Then I was horrified. Had I killed my babies? They had often played on top of John when he was lying down. . . . Where were my babies? I ran to the kitchen. There they were. They seemed terrified. I swept them up in my arms, called my brother to tell him I needed him, and ran to the bathroom with the babies. I locked the door in a panic and huddled on the floor with my babies sobbing. That's where they found me."

When Rose's brother arrived, he found John dead. He notified the police and Rose was taken into custody. She appeared confused and wrung out and was led away limply. She cried only when her babies were taken from her.

When Rose's story was pieced together, the truthfulness of her description seemed irrefutable. A majority of psychiatrists would almost surely agree with a diagnosis of a schizophrenic panic state and legal insanity. But juries are composed of laymen, and adroit prosecuting attorneys have been known to cast doubt on the most psychiatrically sound testimony. All the foregoing was hearsay evidence at best, obtained exclusively from Rose and therefore legally suspect. Perhaps the present signs of psychosis were due to the shock of the crime and did not precede the act.

The telephone call was crucial—that one-chance-in-a-million telephone call. If her girl friend, Pearl, was perceptive and had a good memory, we would have corroborating evidence from an objective source of Rose's state of mind fifteen minutes *before* the crime. This would be a rare stroke of good fortune. Rose's attorney was notified and an appointment promptly made with Pearl. Steps were taken to ensure no prior contact by the two women to avoid any implication of collusion as well as to prevent any contamination of Pearl's observations.

The interview with Pearl was conducted with barely concealed apprehension. Leading questions had to be avoided at all cost or a golden opportunity could be lost irretrievably. Pearl's verbatim replies were transcribed precisely. My fears proved groundless. She turned out to be a pearl of rare luster indeed. She remembered calling Rose at exactly 10:15 A.M. on the morning in question. She had been struck particularly by the length of time the phone rang, at least twenty rings, before it was answered. She had been on the verge of giving up several times but persisted only because she knew Rose was invariably home at that time. Rose finally answered "But there was no expression in her voice, no feeling, no intonation. Nothing. She just replied in one or two words to my questions. That's most unlike her as she usually talks much more than I and bubbles over with all sorts of questions. She sounded so mechanical and preoccupied. She was nowhere near as animated as usual. But the most remarkable thing about that call was the stillness, even over the phone. Everything was so quiet. There were no background noises. Even the canary was silent. I call her every few days at the same time, during our coffee break at work, so I know how much noise there usually is from the bird and the children. That day there was nothing, no movement, no sounds, nothing. It was weird. I remember feeling vaguely uneasy for some time after hanging up."

That was sufficient. It was as perceptive a description of a state of confusion, perplexity, and semistupor and the effect of such a state on children and even on a bird as one could desire.

From a medico-legal point of view from here on it was all downhill. Accordingly, my conclusions that Rose was seriously disturbed and especially that she was an acute suicidal risk were transmitted to her attorney. He requested jail officials to observe her closely. By this time Rose had become a pet of the matrons, clinging to one after another. A few days later while assisting a matron cleaning a second-story tier of cells, she suddenly dashed down the corridor and flung herself over the railing to plunge to the concrete floor below. A guard standing almost directly below was frozen into immobility and reacted seconds too late to break her fall. He said her face in flight appeared enraptured for the first time in her weeks of confinement. She seemed like a giant butterfly which suddenly folds its wings and flutters swiftly to earth.

Rose sustained comminuted fractures of both heels and assorted lacerations. She was promptly hospitalized and recovered satisfactorily. Spurred perhaps by subtly veiled threats of a possible lawsuit from Rose's attorney because of negligence following his warnings concerning her suicidal potential, the legal authorities moved swiftly. She was transferred to a state mental hospital, where she received a course of electroshock treatments with excellent results.

In reviewing Rose's story one is again struck by the realization that to her murder was incidental. For one thing, Rose probably was teetering on the brink of suicide when she held John's gun in her hand for those endless, benumbed minutes. If John had not cried out and startled her, she might have, in T. S. Eliot's words, from "The Love Song of J. Alfred Prufrock":

> *. . . lingered in the chambers of the sea*
> *By sea-girls wreathed with seaweed red and brown*
> *Till human voices wake us and we drown.*

But a human voice did wake her, and she did drown in a sea of overwhelming reality and rage for which she was unprepared and against which she *had* to strike out in a murderous, lifesaving way. She actually murdered John in order to preserve the lives of herself and her babies. Keeping in mind how close Rose had come to committing a double murder and suicide shortly before the actual murder, one wonders if a divine purpose was operating here. Certainly immediately after the murder, Rose was more concerned over almost murdering her babies than over having actually murdered her husband. This single fact, more than any other, was proof of her psychotic state of confusion.

In later years whenever I reflected on Rose's tragic story, the image of her as a fluttering, helpless butterfly kept recurring. I thought of David Belasco's play *Madame Butterfly,* which Puccini converted into his beautiful opera. At first comparisons between the two stories seemed remote. Essentially, though, Rose's murder of her errant husband was the outcome of an aborted suicide.

So, too, Madame Butterfly, in her Oriental frame of reference, by the ritual hara-kiri, symbolically murdered her married lover, Lieutenant Pinkerton. By her act of laying her death on his doorstep, he would "lose face" forever, and be worse than dead because irrevocably dishonored. Since Lieutenant Pinkerton would have to live on with this crushing humiliation, Madame Butterfly was symbolically more vengeful than my poor butterfly.

And So to Court

Eighteen months after John's death, an attractive, fashionably dressed, young matron with a slight limp walked into my office. This woman bore only a remote resemblance to the Rose I had known in jail. She had thirty additional pounds well distributed on her youthful frame, smiled easily, spoke animatedly, and expressed her deeply felt emotions with candor and assurance. She had spent nine months in a state mental hospital receiving a full course of electroshock therapy. Following this there had been a marked alleviation of her depression and a healthy reintegration of her disorganized personality defenses. Her temporary psychosis was adjudged cured by the medical staff. The prosecuting attorney had dismissed the charges against her without a formal hearing, thus sparing Rose a humiliating public ordeal. This was not only justice from a medico-legal point of view but justice tempered with mercy. It was a particularly significant gesture inasmuch as the state-appointed psychiatrist, who had examined Rose in jail before her suicide attempt and had concurred completely with the opinions of the two defense psychiatrists, had died suddenly a few weeks after submitting his report. One could visualize the difficulties a new state psychiatrist would have detecting any lingering signs of psychosis in this composed young lady.

Rose remembered only fragments of the events on the fateful day eighteen months previous. The crucial words came out again in spite of the amnesia-provoking effect of electroshock therapy: "I can remember aiming the gun into the room and firing, but not seeing anything else. The next thing I remember is asking my brother, 'Where are the children?' He said I had told them to go into the kitchen before it happened." She smiled broadly. "I was so relieved. I was afraid I could have killed the children." And so out of the depths of her unconscious, like a phoenix rising out of the ashes of a burned-out conflagration of homicidal-suicidal impulses, came confirmation of the initial impression. To Rose the murder was incidental. By the merest chance another modern-day Medea seemed to have been diverted from the near tragedy that could have sacrificed three lives instead of one. On a deeper level, however, the psychodynamics of her morbidly dependent character structure precisely determined the victim.

The Illness

Oskar Diethelm in Arthur A. Noyes' *Modern Clincial Psychiatry* defines a panic state as "not just a high degree of fear, but a fear based on prolonged tension with a sudden climax which is characterized by fear, extreme insecurity, suspiciousness, and a tendency to projection and disorganization. . . . Because of the underlying sense of insecurity the patient may react with self-assertion, aggressiveness, may rush about or, in other cases, exhibit dilated pupils and the other usual sympathicotonic manifestations of great fear yet remain immobile because he does not dare move. There is often difficulty in thinking and at times a sense and appearance of bewilderment. The reaction usually contains both affective and schizophrenic features, the latter often including considerable disorganization of the personality. Suicide is not uncommon in panic states."

Rose demonstrated a classic picture of the evolution of increasing frustration, anxiety, fear, confusion, and helplessness culminating in the onset of an intense panic state. This rather compliant, dependent individual was blocked in every avenue of assistance she explored. Well-meaning but superficial advice which was either unacceptable to her or too long delayed was offered by her family physician, an attorney, a priest, her brothers, her mother-in-law, and finally by the police. Her personality defenses were primarily centered on dependence upon a stronger figure, and during five years with an immature, detached, arrogant, at times cruel, and enormously uncommunicative, alcoholic husband, these dependency needs were not only inadequately met but trampled upon.

As is typical of morbidly dependent individuals, one of the striking facets of her personality was an inability to express or even to experience hate. At the very moment of firing the gun, Rose did not recognize her anger toward her husband. Most of the other persons involved in her life expressed disgust, dismay, or contempt for her alcoholic husband; she alone felt pity for him. It is indicative of the gradual decompensation of her personality defenses that the night before the crime she had reached the limit of her endurance and at last called the police. When they, too, offered no assistance, this brief upsurge of anger was again repressed, setting off the panic state that ensued the next morning.

Rose's description of her state of mind that morning is that of a panic state of a true psychosis. Here is no simulated temporary insanity where the "mind goes blank and nothing is remembered" until the individual "comes to" with smoking gun in hand. On the contrary, Rose struggled desperately and sincerely to reconstruct and describe a period in time for which there was no prototype in her experience except for one episode of recovering from a fainting spell. She recalled the agitation, the psychomotor restlessness, the tremulousness of that morning, and then the sudden metamorphosis into quietness. The quietness, the inertia, the dazed, stuporous, timeless, bewildering nothingness was described as only a person can who has lived through it. For this was true, naked psychosis, not the simulated psychosis of the malingerer who conceives of it as a complete blanking out of consciousness, for it is no such thing. This was the true fragmentation of the ego, in which sensory perceptions register but in a distorted, vague, and timeless way, and voluntary actions are performed automatically and without true attention or interest. As Harry Stack Sullivan, an authority on schizophrenia, describes it: "All organized activity is lost. All thought is paralyzed. Panic is in fact disorganization of the personality. It arises from the utterly unforeseen failure of something completely trusted and vital for one's safety. Some essential aspect of the universe which one had long taken for granted, suddenly collapses; the disorganization that follows is probably the most appalling state that man undergoes. *Panic is a transitory state and a state wholly incompatible with life."* It is also a state in which one's essential sense of self seems to drop out from under one's feet and one is confronted with nothingness: a truly unendurable catastrophe. Rose was fortunate that corroboration of her dazed state was available from an objective source—her friend Pearl. At the time Rose wandered to the bureau she could have been going for the babies' diapers or to get the gun; it is doubtful if Rose will ever know for certain. And it is even less certain whether she was about to commit murder or suicide. It is my strong suspicion that suicide was much more likely, but at the crucial moment her husband roused from his sleep and startled her. It is a time-honored axiom in psychiatry: never touch physically or startle with any loud or unexpected movement a person in a panic state. The explosive and unpredictable outburst of homicidal or suicidal impulses is all too likely. Thus it was in this case and a life was sacrificed. Immediately afterward she grabbed her children and huddled in the bathroom in abject terror; terror of her *own* hostile, uncontrolled impulses. The tragic irony is that such a compliant, dependent person who never expresses anger is more vulnerable than most of us to a sudden explosive breakthrough of hostile impulses. Her defenses, seemingly impervious to anything, were actually brittle from long abuse, and they shattered completely when the stresses of life overwhelmed her. Another indication of her true state of disorganization was her horror at the thought that she might have killed her children, who often played on their father when he was asleep on the sofa. It is an example of her dazed and distorted state of perception that she could have fired indiscriminately and uncontrollably without recognizing their presence. And well she might have. This probably explains her clinging to the children in such terrified relief when she saw them in the kitchen afterward. Parenthetically, the explanation for the abnormal quietness of the children during her stuperous panic state is undoubtedly that they sensed something was wrong with their mother and froze in terror themselves. Children, particularly at the preverbal stage of development, like animals, figuratively "breathe" in an atmosphere of feelings as no adult can. Although they could not understand her state of mind, they *knew* something was radically wrong and remained mute and immobile throughout.

Rose's statement that her dazed state disappeared as her husband shouted at her and "then everything was real. It was so real . . ." was all too accurate. With the act of violence the state of disorganization or schizophrenic panic was temporarily aborted. She was literally shocked back to reality, much as in medieval times it was standard procedure to immerse witches, who may well have been schizophrenics, in water almost to the point of drowning. Thus the devil would be exorcised, and in fact many such wretches were "cured" by the overwhelming impact of threatening reality. So, too, this psychotic state was aborted from its usual aftermath, which is the development of pathological delusions and hallucinations. These latter symptoms are actually restorative phenomena, attempts of the organism to account for the appalling and bewildering state of ego disillusion or nothingness in some reasonable way. Although the hallucinations are often insane-seeming to the objective observer, they are actually attempts at a healthy reintegration of the personality with reality, a healing of the breach in the ego defenses, a solution to the terrifying not-knowing that is so intolerable. But such an act of violence determines a different outcome: the establishment of an intense depression, partly due to a distressing external reality but mostly due to inner emotional conflicts. In this case it converted a basically schizophrenic state of the schizo-affective type into a depressive reaction, also of psychotic proportions, but one in which the elements of schizophrenic disorganization were somewhat masked by the depression.

Why Did It Happen?

Rose, a characteristically self-effacing person, had originally established an intensely morbidly dependent relationship with her husband. As the latter deteriorated steadily into chronic alcoholism, this equilibrium became more and more unstable until it reached the point of breakdown. Her neurotic pride, invested in constancy of a loving relationship and glorification of the capacity to endure any abuse, was temporarily shattered. She was thrust into the position of assuming greater responsibility. Her frantic last-minute groping for support from priest, physician, relatives, psychiatrist, and attorney were of no avail. Finally, after one particularly abusive assault by her husband, she "had had it," and made her precipitous move toward healthy assertiveness. She called the police to arrest her husband. When this unaccustomed behavior was not immediately reinforced and bolstered by the police, she plunged into a state of enormous panic and indecision. Immersion in this unstable, precarious new position of self-assertion, which clashed irrevocably with her habitual self-effacement, produced intense conflict to the point of disorganization. When John awoke and startled her while she was musing over the gun, she was suddenly galvanized into action and lurched back to her former position of psychic safety by annihilating the one person who had seemingly prevented her from making her original neurotic solution work. She also struck out at the person who had almost driven her to the point of murdering her two children and then killing herself. After John's death she could then reconstitute her dependency on her physician, attorney, jail matrons, and so forth. When even this new-found state of dependency did not allay her anxiety sufficiently, she attempted suicide to efface herself completely. Failing in this, she did, however, succeed in rendering herself so injured and helpless as to necessitate being treated even more wholeheartedly in a hospital ward. At last she would be cared for and her need for unconditional love, tenderness, and sympathy would be fulfilled, if only temporarily.

Some Personal Reflections

Rose was the first person accused of murder whom I ever examined as a psychiatrist. She was such a pitiful, bewildered waif, so atypical of the stereotyped, overly aggressive murderer, so obviously overwhelmed by years of neglect and abuse by her husband, that no one, including the state prosecutors, appeared to be clamoring for vengeance. Even several of her former in-laws were reported to be sympathetic to her plight. The atmosphere surrounding the pretrial investigation seemed more compatible with deliberate, measured exploration of her psychiatric condition than in more sharply adversarial cases.

However, since it was my initial experience with medico-legal procedures, I was apprehensive about certifying to her legal insanity without more spectacular and definitive signs of psychosis. Some conveniently discovered hallucinations or delusions of being poisoned by her husband, for instance, would have provided a more solid basis upon which to build a convincing picture of severe mental pathology to present to a jury of lay people. I was particularly concerned that the signs of her mental illness could be interpreted as occurring *after* and in response to the crime rather than preceding and contributing to it. The fortunate circumstance of her friend Pearl's having talked to her on the phone minutes before the shooting was the rock upon which her psychiatric defense would rest.

Fortunately from a medico-legal but unfortunately from a self-preservative point of view, Rose's serious suicidal attempt eliminated any potentially hazardous testing of that defense. No one involved in the disposition of her case needed further proof of the depth of her despair or the authenticity of her profound personality disorganization. A malingerer she was not.

The further misfortune of the death of the state-appointed psychiatrist after he had examined Rose and found her seriously ill would have possibly complicated legal proceedings even more. The presence of humane men and women of good will on both sides of the legal conflict produced an outcome with which, I feel, most fair-minded people would agree. It is quite likely that Rose has suffered and will continue to suffer intense inner anguish over her act for the rest of her life.

Because Rose was judged innocent by reason of insanity, she received her husband's insurance as the legitimate beneficiary. (If she had been found guilty, she would have lost all claim to the money since a person cannot legally profit from his or her crimes.) She used the funds to support her children and herself while supplementing this income with part-time employment.

After reading Rose's tragic story, perhaps you may have begun moving in the direction of suspecting, as I have, if only at times and if only in part, even with those who have committed this irrevocable crime, that if we could *truly* understand all, we could forgive all.

Summary

Tell all the truth but tell it slant . . .
With explanation kind.
The truth must dazzle gradually
Or every man be blind.
—Emily Dickinson

PSYCHOANALYSIS AND PSYCHODYNAMICALLY ORI-
ented psychotherapy have been described as slow,
arduous, and painful processes of disillusionment in
that they involve the gradual undermining of the illusions of
childhood. This is a cornerstone of Karen Horney's thinking.
She feels children who are particularly anxious due to destructive, unfeeling, or hypocritical early life experiences adopt
defensive devices to survive on the best terms possible with
their limited psychological resources. These are maneuvers of
expediency, to alleviate anxiety, rather than measures of personal satisfaction leading to ultimate and self-fulfilling values.
She distinguishes between two separate and mutually exclusive directions of growth: that toward self-idealization
and that toward self-realization.

Self-idealization is a movement away from one's immanent human potential. It aims toward spurious goals, toward *pretensions* rather than actualities. Self-idealization, as Karen Horney outlined it, is a dirty word to describe a destructive way of life. It is this neurotic way of life that is basic to all emotional or mental illnesses as she understood them. Unfortunately, "idealization" is too easily confused with "idealistic" or "ideals"—emotive words of entirely different, even opposite, connotations.

Horney's theories, as well as those of Harry Stack Sullivan, Erich Fromm, and other neo-Freudian psychoanalysts, all suffer somewhat by their terminology. They have been accused of superficiality for dealing with the ego as opposed to the reputedly more searching exploration of the id by Freudian psychoanalysts. Without going into any polemics on these differences of opinion, I feel the use of language may contribute to this misunderstanding. "Self-idealization" does not produce the immediate impact of words like "castration anxiety," "anality," "death instinct," or "incestuous Oedipal strivings." Even if many of the latter concepts are no longer especially helpful in psychoanalytic thinking, they still resonate splendidly through the chambers of the mind.

One of the purposes of this book is to attempt to put some exclamation marks after the concept of self-idealization. Self-idealization is carried out unconsciously by the child's developing of an "idealized self-image." This sick self-image is insidiously developed at an early age and gradually evolves almost as if with a will of its own. It is honed and elaborated with each passing year. It serves to smooth out contradictions in one's personality and thus to keep the anxiety resulting from underlying emotional conflicts from emerging precipitously or unbearably.

Nobody develops neurotic defenses unless he or she needs them. It is no one's favorite indoor sport nor a way to relieve one's boredom. To unravel these defenses, to reverse a disturbed person's directions from unhealthy pretensions to genuine living with authentic goals and ideals is a struggle of considerable magnitude. Playwrights Arthur Miller in *Death of a Salesman,* Eugene O'Neill in *The Iceman Cometh,* and Edward Albee in *Who's Afraid of Virginia Woolf?* attempted to destroy cherished illusions with swift, surgical precision. Their plays dramatically illustrate the hazards implicit in such precipitate actions. Psychoanalysts particularly recognize the futility as well as the dangers of such haste. Emperor Augustus's admonition "Make haste slowly" is the correct procedure in attempting to alter underlying personality traits.

This group of murderers and near-murderers had idealized themselves in metaphors of fairy-tale characters. They had aggrandized themselves in fashions appropriate to childhood. Unfortunately, reality in the form of adult responsibilities and expectations intruded suddenly and unexpectedly. Their fantasy-like self-images collapsed temporarily. They found themselves thrust into unendurable states of conflicting emotions, often to the point of disintegration of the organized sense of self. From these positions of unexpected panic and turmoil they improvised rapidly and impulsively. Scapegoats were chosen, persecutors accused, or the most readily available victims selected. Murder occurred in each individual's single-minded rush back to his or her familiar psychic position of spurious safety. Everyone should reserve for himself or herself the inalienable right to survive on whatever terms are necessary—but not at the cost of another's life.

These murderers and near-murderers seemed on the surface to have committed "incidental" murders. It was only by remaining open to these individuals' personalized, unique frames of reference, by working from within outward, that I saw these murders as being anything but incidental. They were absolutely essential to the murderers' psychic existences at a specific moment in time and space. Owing to certain chains of events and stimuli, unstable psychodynamic equilibriums in these individuals were disrupted or shattered. These bewildered, frightened, isolated, and severely alienated individuals were trying to "recover" from intolerable states of turmoil and intense, disintegrating conflict into which they had been plunged without warning or comprehension. In their frenzy to reestablish previously more tolerable, albeit unhealthy, states of psychic equilibriums, most sacrificed a human life.

In many of these individuals one or both of two psychodynamically significant events took place. These two events overlapped and are concomitants, but with each individual one element may appear more verifiable. The first was a shattering blow dealt to the individual's neurotic pride system, triggering off enormously intense self-hate. This anger was externalized to the victim and abated only after his removal by the act of murder, which allowed a temporary shoring up of the unstable pride system. The second was a radical move away from a formerly held major "neurotic solution" to a hitherto repressed solution, such as from expansiveness to self-effacement in Juan, or in the opposite direction in Rose. This move was too precipitous and ill-prepared and could not be sustained, setting off intense, overpowering conflict with inevitable anxiety, often to a panic degree. The murderous impulse annihilated the victim, who was inadvertently obstructing the murderer as he or she scurried frantically back to the pseudosafety of the more familiar neurotic solution.

Many of these individuals described a point of no return when they felt they had to do something other than what they had been doing. Robin recognized he had been relieving the wrong people of their money and had to restrict himself to robbing banks. Once he had the bank's money, "they" had to remain silent. Peter landed briefly in the world of responsibility and married. The strain of this unaccustomed intimacy contributed to increasing drinking and careless driving. Ned forsook his vaunted cool detachment and acted out his antagonism toward authorities. Juan discovered Carmelita in a blatantly compromising situation, beat her unmercifully, recognized the utter futility of his actions, and moved to the uncharacteristic position of placating, cajoling, and begging her forgiveness. Thomas relaxed his vigilance against physical violation and then exploded several times. Otto sensed Eloise's yearning for affection and nurturing and sought drunkenly and simplistically to fulfill it through sexual means. Dan betrayed his covenant with God that permitted him to steal with impunity and assisted an accomplice's homicidal acts. Rose gazed up at her husband for a long, long moment after he had assaulted her; she "had had it." She then called the police and felt something important settled in her mind. Most, in essence, described some momentous, earthshaking event which had specific meaning in relationship to the basic, unique character structure of each.

In their clumsy, ill-conceived, but characterologically consistent attempts at striving for their unique "goods," they all moved precipitously. As with a sudden military advance, extensive and well-organized supporting supplies are crucial for the maintenance of the combat troops. The point of foremost penetration is the position of greatest hazard as well as heroism. All will end disastrously, however, if the unspectacular, patient, foot-slogging consolidation maneuvers are not performed in timely and satisfactory fashion in the rear. In these unfortunate individuals such was not done. Their sudden surges toward change produced overwhelming conflict and increasing anxiety, often to the point of disorganization and panic. They then lunged impulsively back toward "lines of departure," to their status quo, to their habitual, safer psychic positions. The victims were frequently symbolic impediments to those wild lunges and consequently were eliminated.

Karl Augustus Menninger's paper, "Murder Without Apparent Motive," offers a selection of cases somewhat different from these. However, the article states, ". . . when such apparently senseless murders occur they are seen to be an end result of a period of increasing tension and disorganization in the murderer starting before contact with the victim, who, by fitting into the unconscious conflicts of the murderer, unwittingly serves to set into motion his homicidal potential." My observations do not contradict this statement as much as expand it. The victims set off conflicts which, through the insights of Horney's theory, may be seen to be of such magnitude as to threaten the entire unstable neurotic structure. The idealized images and neurotic pride systems of the murderers are shaken to their foundations, provoking the self-hate which, as Horney said, ". . . is not only a split, but a cruel and murderous battle." These individuals confirm the accuracy and perspicacity of her prediction. It can indeed be murderous. So, too, the victims did not seem merely to "fit into the unconscious conflicts" but were rather a symbolic or actual impediment to the imperative return of the murderers to their characteristic neurotic solutions. Therefore, they *had* to be eliminated.

There is a consistent theme of blatant self-destructiveness that runs through the stories of these individuals, along with a seeming indifference to their own lives. Robin flipped a cigarette at a judge and attempted suicide several times as a youth. Peter was as careless with his own life as with his wife's in his drunken driving. Ned refused to entertain an insanity plea in order to retain the respect of his family as well as to deprive the police of the satisfaction of arresting the true culprit. Juan was indifferent to possible execution as long as he could preserve his secret from ridicule. Thomas would strike out at armed prison guards when inadvertently touched. Otto threatened suicide in attempting to save his unborn children. Dan had attempted suicide many times in state mental hospitals and wished fervently to be killed in order to return from the dead. Rose attempted suicide by gas before her homicide as well as plunging from a jail tier afterwards. It would seem that a hopelessness and contempt for one's own life is a common precursor to the act of taking another's life.

All these individuals were exceedingly estranged from their own inner feelings, especially in regard to feelings of anger. It was remarkable how defenseless they all were in their attempts not to excuse but even to explain and account for why they had killed. Each chapter in this book is an organized summary of many hours of seemingly aimless, frustrating, and bewildering meanderings over, under, and around the events leading up to the crimes and the inner responses of these individuals. They were so alienated from their feelings that they were helpless to connect their own emotions with their violent acts. They were especially vulnerable to the sudden outbreak of their rage because of almost total unawareness of the gradual crescendo within. They were strangers imprisoned within their own skins and subjected to volcanic eruptions of unpredictable direction and force. You have to touch, share, and own before you can control.

Each individual manifested a sense of isolation and loneliness that frequently reached its acme shortly before the crime. Each had very distant interpersonal relations, with an inordinate emotional investment in one other human being. When these unique relationships were disrupted, the sense of isolation became complete and unbearable.

The key to recognizing severe emotional illness in each individual lay in some overwhelming passion which took precedence over murder. The psychiatrist approaches the murderer with the unspoken assumption that the latter will regard this ultimate crime with the same intense emotional response as would the psychiatrist, were the positions reversed. In these instances, such was not the case. As the murderer's hierarchy of values emerged, it was apparent that some other value occupied the place usually reserved for respect for human life. This value, exaggerated and distorted though it may have been, was incorporated in the idealized self-image and represented the very essence of the individual. It was invariably invested with intense emotional force. Without this inner core the murderer faced psychic annihilation in his personal, inner frame of reference. Robert Ruark, in *Something of Value,* quoted this Basuto proverb, "If a man does away with his traditional way of living and throws away his good customs, he had better make certain that he has something of value to replace them." In these instances such was not possible. Even murder, the ultimate crime against one's fellow man, will be committed in order to sustain those ideas that seem crucial to the person's existence. Robin was consumed with his magnificent delusion for redressing all the iniquities of the world; an uncooperative bank official was an unexpected but trivial annoyance. Peter was obsessed with the temporary ridiculousness of his position after the car accident; the death of his wife and unborn child were of minor import. Ned's assertion of his inalienable right to be overlooked justified overlooking his murder of a policeman. Juan was preoccupied with his forthcoming marriage to Carmelita now that she at last recognized and respected his manliness. Thomas's absolute control over his life space permitted no intrusion, however inadvertent. Otto was more preoccupied with a fantasied murder than with his actual crime. He was also more guilt-ridden over child molesting than child murder. God's special covenant with Dan took precedence over the fate of any mere mortal. Rose was more frightened by the possibility of having harmed her children than by the actuality of killing her husband. It was these points of focus which, when discovered and followed respectfully and without preconceptions, led to the heart of their idealized images. Murder was incidental compared to the maintenance of these inner values.

In reality these inner values were not genuine, authentic virtues of these individuals. They were compounded of more pretense than substance. They were qualities *arrogated* to them by their imaginations. Robin's beneficence was a device to gain affection from other unfortunates. Peter's boyish charm and ready wit were designed to distract one from the shallow, utterly selfish boy-that-never-grew-up underneath. Ned's cherished respect was actually his demand for unrestricted privileges in all circumstances and for all time. Juan's machismo actually concealed a fragile expansiveness which required constant approbation, even from an imbecilic Carmelita. Thomas's physical inviolability was a shield to protect him from his failures at differentiating those who meant him well from those who meant him ill. Otto's Pied Piper posture toward children developed as an overcompensation for the discomfort he experienced in dealing with his own peers. Dan's hallucinatory commands compensated for his feelings of inadequacy and suggestibility to the wills of others. Rose's overriding maternal protectiveness actually masked a profound morbid dependency. Her rage toward her husband was fundamentally due to his failure to support those extreme dependency needs. These underlying, powerful neurotic trends, disguised though they might be by idealizing labels by the persons concerned, were their unacceptable personal attributes. At all cost they *had* to be hidden from the world and themselves.

All these murders were useless. Though each murderer was striving for a greater "good" within his or her distorted scale of values, no permanent solution was obtained. Their self-images and personalities were simply too shaky to withstand the buffetings of time and events. They all resorted to murder in order magically to produce an ultimate, permanent solution to all their psychic problems. A disorganized, anxiety-ridden individual will reach out frantically for the pat, simplistic, unitary, seemingly all-inclusve answer. What is hoped for is the once-and-for-all-time triumph over all of life's uncertainties and conflicts. To the murderers in their respective states of panic, the victims appeared to be the main obstacle to the attainment of their immediate goals, and in fact the culmination of committing their crimes did afford a temporary surcease from terror. Inevitably, though, the punitive self-doubts recurred. Since the murderers' problems were invariably due to their own hidden emotional conflicts, to the inner chafing under the whips of their own unyielding expectations and "shoulds," the removal of scapegoats was of no lasting avail.

Like the measured tread of a Greek tragedy, the life of each of these less-than-heroic, but nevertheless tortured, conflicted individuals moved inexorably to the ultimate denouement of a human death. Just as in the case of those Greek tragic heroes who suffered from hubris, or overreaching pride, so the rigid, narrow-based, unbending neurotic pride systems of these individuals led them to fatal violence. They, too, wrestled with the gods, but it was with their private, inner godlike images of themselves. Their perfectionistic exaggerations proved their undoing. They demonstrated only too clearly that perfect is the enemy of the good.

In Homer's *Iliad* there are two concurrent levels of conflict: the secondary combat among the mortals on the plains of Troy and the primary conflict among the immortals on Mount Olympus. So, too, these murders seemed of only incidental import to these persons compared to the intensity of their inner conflicts. Their greater "goods" reposed in metaphorical, otherworldly spheres. Human life weighed lightly on such scales.

One of Horney's earliest and most fundamental insights into human nature was that anxiety and hostility were intimately and inextricably intertwined in the neurotic character structure. The vicious feedback of anxiety leading to diffuse hostility which led to more anxiety causing further hostility shed light on the enormous quantity of anger clinically evident in the intricacies of neurotic entanglements. This is epitomized by the Russian proverb: "Master of one's own anger, master of all." These persons, obsessed with their private self-idealizations and neurotic prides, steadily weakened their real selves in their destructive, driven quests for spurious goals. Any real efforts to master their own inner conflicts, particularly their conflicts over hostility, were lost in the neurotic underbrush. Gentleness, which tentatively emerged in many of them at times, was deeply distrusted by many of them. They confused it with weakness, fearing it might open them to greater vulnerability to others. They were almost totally blind to the truth that most mature individuals finally attain. As Dr. Alexander Reid Martin has said, "Only the strong can be gentle. Only the arrogant can be weak."

These people were particularly predisposed to homicidal furies because they had secretly idealized themselves in grandiose fashion. They had raised certain personality traits, certain "goods," certain values to transcendent heights while ignoring or denying the importance of opposing or mitigating factors. They defended themselves with only one or two arrows in their quivers. They strove unconsciously to survive by means of illusory simplifying formulas—"The trick is not to care" or "The trick is to love someone totally" or "The trick is to be so powerful others will fear you." But life is hardly ever amenable to such tricks. It has to be experienced intensely, appropriately, and authentically, with a mind open to the eternal fascination of its diversity and a heart open to its pain as well as its joy, for without accepting the pain one cannot reach out for the joy. It is only by remaining open and tentative in the face of confusion, by maintaining an inner flexibility in the face of changing customs, changing conditions, and changing people that one can grow and expand. Stubbornness of mind, meanness of spirit, foolish consistency, misplaced simplification, and rigidity of response lead to neurotic impoverishment and, as with these individuals, tragic outcomes.

Few indeed ever live out their destinies on their own terms.

Appendix

A Survey of Karen Horney's Theories

> The neurotic process
> [parallels the mythological
> devil's pact]: an individual in
> psychic distress arrogates to
> himself infinite powers,
> losing his soul, and suffering
> the torments of hell in his
> self-hate.
> —Karen Horney

KAREN HORNEY (1885-1952) PRACTICED AND TAUGHT THE theories and techniques of Freudian psychoanalysis for more than fifteen years. Her dissatisfaction with therapeutic results combined with doubts about Freud's views on feminine psychology led her to an extensive revision of psychoanalytic theory. The heterogeneity of personality types she found in America, as contrasted to her native Germany, opened her eyes to the possibility that cultural and interpersonal factors weighed more heavily in an individual's psychic development than the more universal biological factors emphasized by Freud. She retained the fundamentals of Freud's psycho-analytic concepts, namely "that psychic processes are strictly determined, that actions and feelings may be determined by unconscious motivations, and that the motivations that drive us are emotional forces." Eventually she rejected Freud's instinctivistic orientation, including his libido theory and the death instinct; the repetition compulsion; the concepts of innate destructiveness and dualities; his belief that the scientific attitude excludes moral valuation; and most of all, what she considered his pessimistic philosophy. Instead she optimistically and humanistically believed "in the inner dignity and freedom of man and in the constructiveness of the evolutionary forces inherent in man."

The real self came to occupy the dynamic core of her view of human personality. This was "the central inner force common to all human beings and yet unique in each, which is the deep source of healthy growth." It is the self "we refer to when we say that we want to find ourselves." The real self is the source of our capacities for experiencing and expressing our alive, spontaneous feelings, for taking responsibility for our actions and their consequences, and for evolving our own values and making choices based on them. It produces genuine integration, which is a natural process in which all aspects of the individual function harmoniously and without serious inner conflict, giving the individual a solid sense of his realness, his identity, his wholeness. These constructive forces of the real self unfold and develop in the process of healthy growing she termed self-realization.

In diametric opposition to this healthy growth is the neurotic development which she saw as a search for glory, a process of self-idealization. She felt neurotics had two predominant characteristics: a certain rigidity of reaction and a discrepancy between potentialities and accomplishments. They were driven in various situations to act compulsively instead of being free to choose and therefore often responded inappropriately.

Crucial to her understanding of the genesis of neurosis was the concept of basic anxiety. According to her belief, a child exposed to unhealthy nurturing figures, who were indifferent or hostile to the child's legitimate needs and wishes, smothered it with guilt-inducing "love," coerced, exploited, and above all treated him inconsistently and hypocritically, developed basic anxiety. He felt helpless and alone in a potentially hostile world. To cope with this menacing world, the child developed neurotic character trends. These trends developed out of three possible attitudes toward people. When moving *toward* people, the child accepted his own helplessness, and in spite of his estrangement and fears tried to win the affection of others and to lean on them. When he moved *against* people, he accepted and took for granted the hostility around him, and determined, consciously or unconsciously, to fight. When he moved *away from* people, he wanted neither to belong nor to fight but to keep apart. In each of these attitudes one of the elements involved in the basic anxiety was emphasized; helplessness in the first, hostility in the second, and isolation in the third. In the normal person the three attitudes are not felt as mutually exclusive. The three can complement each other and make for a harmonious whole. This, however, cannot happen in neurotics because neurotic trends are compulsive, indiscriminate, insatiable, and contradictory. Further, what began with the family extends to all future relationships and to life in general. Ultimately the entire personality is pervaded.

Horney felt that conflict born of incompatible attitudes constitutes the core of neurosis and therefore deserves to be called basic conflict. It is the dynamic center from which neuroses emanate. This contention is the nucleus of a new theory of neurosis: that neuroses are an expression of a disturbance in human relationships.

Horney classifies these three attitudes as the *compliant* (toward), the *aggressive* (against), and the *detached* (away from) personalities. In each type the basic attitude toward others has created or at least fostered the growth of certain needs, qualities, sensitivities, inhibitions, anxieties, and, last but not least, a particular set of values. There are no pure forms, but in many neurotics one attitude will predominate and be more acceptable to, and characteristic of, the individual. However, the other two attitudes are always there.

The neurotic individual uses four methods to "solve" (rather than "resolve") the basic conflict. In the first case, he represses certain aspects of his personality, and their opposites are brought to the foreground. In the second method he creates an artificial harmony by detachment, even though detachment is also an element in the basic conflict. In the third case he defuses conflicts by creating an "idealized image"—what the neurotic believes he is, can, or ought to be. We see this most obviously in the grandiose notions of psychosis, but the idealized image can be considered as a bit of psychosis woven into the texture of neurosis. Though an imaginative, unconscious creation, it is determined by realistic factors. As he becomes sicker, the neurotic experiences increasing alienation from his real self and to him his idealized image becomes reality. Created to solve conflict, it generates further tensions, requiring a fourth attempt at solution—externalization. Externalization is the tendency to experience internal processes as if they occurred outside oneself and, as a rule, to hold these external factors responsible for one's difficulties. Although idealization was a move away from the real self, it was still within the confines of the self. Externalization means departing from the territory of self altogether.

Unresolved conflicts inevitably lead to moral impairment. The neurotic's ideals no longer have obligating powers for his life, producing insincerity and egocentricity. Unconscious pretenses, counterfeits of authentic ideals, are developed. Among them are the pretenses of goodness, of love, of honesty and fairness, of suffering, etc. He also develops unconscious arrogance, meaning arrogating to oneself qualities one does not have or that one has in a lesser degree than assumed, and of unconsciously claiming the right on this ground to be demanding and derogatory towards others. Coupled with moral impairment is the inability to take a definite stand and consequent undependability. A person cannot be genuinely responsible if he does not know what genuine responsibility is. The ultimate product of unresolved conflicts is hopelessness, with its deepest root in the despair of ever being wholehearted and undivided.

To resolve neurotic conflicts properly there is in Horney's opinion only one radical, difficult way—to change those conditions within the personality that brought them into being. It entails the analysis of the entire neurotic character structure. The goals of therapy are that the patient should acquire the capacity to assume responsibility for himself and should achieve an inner independence, spontaneity of feelings, and most comprehensively, wholeheartedness.

The child, goaded by basic anxiety, is forced to develop contradictory and compulsive attitudes toward others. He is, therefore, in basic conflict. To attain some illusory semblance of unity, he becomes predominantly aggressive, compliant, or detached. But this childish, neurotic attempt at integration is not firm enough, necessitating a more comprehensive solution—self-idealization. Through self-idealization the child avoids conflict, gains fulfillment, and identity; but in imagination alone. However, this outcome of an earlier neurotic development sets in motion a new one—the actualizing of the idealized self. This process Horney termed the search for glory.

Although self-idealization remains the nuclear part of the search for glory, other elements are the need for perfection, neurotic ambition, and the need for a vindictive triumph. Although a person may consciously feel he *wants* to attain his standards of perfection, he is actually *driven* to attain them. The compulsiveness of this search is revealed in its indiscriminate nature, its insatiability, its utter disregard for the person's best interests, and in its exaggerated reactions to frustration. Inasmuch as imagination plays such a crucial role in the search for glory and because needs, not wishes, drive him, the neurotic aims at the absolute and the ultimate. The most pertinent symbol for the neurotic process initiated by the search for glory is the ideational content of the stories of the devil's pact repeatedly portrayed in fiction, such as Johann Goethe's *Faust*, Oscar Wilde's *The Picture of Dorian Gray*, and Stephen Vincent Benet's *The Devil and Daniel Webster*. In each a human being in distress reaches for the absolute and godlike, giving up his soul and ending in hell, the hell of his own self-hate. The loss of the soul, to Horney, is the deeper, quieter despair of alienation from the real self. The search for glory has caused the neurotic to become a hated stranger to himself.

Having strayed into the realm of the fantastic, of the infinite, of boundless possibilities, the neurotic turns his needs and wishes into claims. Claims are irrational demands made on reality. They are assumed entitlements based on the neurotic's grandiose notions about himself. "Everyone ought to cater to his illusion. Everything short of this is unfair. . . . Moreover, whatever he feels, thinks, or does ought not to carry any adverse consequences. This means in fact a claim that psychic laws ought not to apply to him." He no longer needs to recognize or change his difficulties; others should see that they do not disturb him. In spite of the impossibility of fulfillment of his claims, he asserts his right to them, even to such frankly fantastic claims as being exempt from illness, old age, and death. To assert his claims is essential. If he continues to uphold them, some day they *must* come true. "The claims are his guarantee for future glory."

Neurotic claims are concerned with the outer world; "shoulds" focus on the inner world of the neurotic. Shoulds comprise all a neurotic should be able to do, to be, to feel, to know, and also taboos on how and what he should not be. "The premise on which they operate is that nothing should be, or is, impossible for oneself." Shoulds are so inexorable and operate with such disregard for their feasibility that Horney called them "the tyranny of the should." They goad the neurotic to actualize his exaggerated self-image of perfection but lack the moral seriousness of genuine ideals. Instead they aim at making imperfections disappear or making it appear *as if* the particular perfection were attained.

"With all his strenuous efforts toward perfection and with all his belief in perfection attained, the neurotic does not gain what he most desperately needs: self-confidence and self-respect. Even though godlike in his imagination, he still lacks the earthy self-confidence of a simple shepherd. . . . And, as in the stories of the devil's pact, he gets all the glory in imagination and sometimes in reality. But instead of solid self-confidence he gets a glittering gift of most questionable value: neurotic pride. . . . Neurotic pride, in all its forms, is false pride." The neurotic trends which serve to actualize the idealized self are the only ones invested with pride. Neurotic pride produces increased vulnerability because it is based on shaky foundations. This produces automatic endeavors to restore pride when it is hurt and to avoid injury when it is endangered. The need to save face when pride is injured often leads to vindictiveness. This vindictiveness is not satisfied by getting even but must triumph and hit back harder, thereby becoming a self-vindication. The neurotic's pride continues to be hurt, however, leading to intense self-hate. Since the flight to glory and its attendant exaggerated pride inevitably produce enormous hate for the actual self, Horney called "the sum total of the factors involved by a common name: the pride system." She was astounded by the enormity and tenacity of self-hate she discovered in neurotics. "Man in reaching out for the infinite and absolute also starts destroying himself."

In the search for glory the neurotic alienates himself from his real self, from his alive center. He becomes remote from his own feelings, wishes, beliefs, and energies. Everything that is compulsive in neurosis drives him further from his core. He becomes a victim of his drives rather than his choices. His relations with himself and all of life become impersonal. Neurotic pride governs his feelings and causes them to be reactive, ill-sustained, and ungenuine. Alienation also weakens one's directive powers in life, the faculty of assuming responsibility for oneself, and ultimately one's spontaneous integrating power.

Finally, the neurotic develops something of an encompassing character to give form and direction to the whole personality. These are the so-called major solutions— expansiveness, self-effacement, and resignation. Each determines the kinds of satisfactions attainable, the persons and situations to be avoided, the hierarchy of values established, the ways that a person will relate to himself and others. While Horney suggests total neurotic structures as a more comprehensive basis for a typology, she warns that the use of types is limited because what is seen is a mixture of types. She feels it would be more correct to speak of directions of development rather than of types.

In the "expansive" solution, where the individual identifies predominantly with his glorified self, the appeal of mastery is what drives him. He is determined to copy with any contingency and is convinced that he can do so successfully. Anything connoting helplessness is his most poignant dread.

There are three subdivisions of the expansive type—narcissistic, perfectionistic, and arrogant-vindictive. The narcissist believes he is his idealized self and adores it. Narcissism thus becomes one of the several solutions of the conflict between expansive and self-effacing drives. The perfectionist identifies with his standards, is constantly straining to fulfill them, and with arrogant contempt looks down on others from the heights of imagined fulfillment. The arrogant-vindictive type identifies with his pride. Although vindictiveness is a regular ingredient in the search for glory and therefore common to all neurotics, in this type it is present in overwhelming intensity and becomes a way of life. Because "for all so-called sadistic trends, vindictive needs are the crucial motivating force." The term vindictive was suggested by Horney as the general term, and sadistic for "the satisfaction to be gained from the power to subject others to pain or indignity."

In the "self-effacing" solution, the appeal of love has the most powerful pull. This type identifies not with his glorified self but with his despised self. Anything suggesting superiority or triumph must be and is shunned. In all its essentials this solution is a move in directions opposite to that of the expansive solution. He constantly shrinks and minimizes himself yet always feels guilty. Life appears possible only under the shadow of someone else—a partner, who will defend him against a hostile world. However, he often does not choose a partner as much as become spell-bound by a stronger, superior individual. He often feels like a stowaway without rights of passage. He suffers from neurotic involvement as do others, and the suffering is genuine. However, the suffering assumes neurotic functions when it is whipped up and used to accuse others and excuse himself. Self-effacement appears to be the least satisfactory of the three major solutions since it makes for greater subjective feelings of unhappiness, aggravated by the many functions suffering serves. Also his needs and expectations make him excessively dependent on people, whom he cannot help but hate because he is so divided. Nevertheless, he persists in maintaining that love solves all. Peace and unity will finally come through love as will the actualizing of his idealized image. Lovableness is cherished in an exaggerated way and he asserts his claims against others because of his compliance or sensitivity or understanding nature. These attributes are often overrated in himself. His "prideful humility" and enormous dependency needs, which he glorifies as the pure gold of lovableness, cause further deterioration in his human relationships. He wallows in abused feelings and often in self-degradation, especially of a sexual nature. Going to pieces and fascination with chronic illnesses frequently appeal to him. Morbid dependency is the end stage of self-effacement.

The third major solution to intrapsychic conflicts is that of "resignation." In resignation the appeal of freedom predominates, but a freedom from, not a freedom for, active living. Such a person becomes a spectator of himself and his life. He no longer strives for achievement and is loath to make efforts. His life lacks goals, direction, and planning. At a deeper level he severely restricts his wishes. His relationships with people become characterized by detachment. Inevitably he becomes hypersensitive to any influence, pressure, coercion, or ties, and adverse to change. Independence and a static insistence on the maintenance of the status quo are his shibboleths. Three different forms of living may result from this neurotic direction of development. In the first group, persistent resignation with all that it entails is carried through fairly consistently. In the rebellious group, the passive resistance can turn into an active rebellion, but a rebellion against, not for. In the third group, deteriorating processes prevail and lead to shallow living, a movement to the periphery of life. The emphasis is placed on fun, having a good time, on prestige, on opportunistic success, or on becoming a well-adapted automaton.

Expansiveness, self-effacement, and resignation as major solutions to basic conflict arise out of and create disturbances in relation to self and to others in life, in work, in love, and in leisure. Whereas previously Horney had defined neurosis as a disturbance in human relationships, she eventually saw it as a "disturbance in one's relation to self and to others" and that the neurotic was "a person in whom neurotic drives prevail over healthy strivings."

Psychiatry has been described as the study of interpersonal distortions. As the neurotic develops an idealized image with its supporting neurotic pride system, shoulds, and claims, he of necessity selects out of the myriad of life experiences those that reinforce his neurotic solution and ignores or minimizes those that contradict it. As Alexander Pope points out, "... all looks yellow to the jaundic'd eye." Accordingly there is a self-perpetuating quality to the neurotic way of life, which tends to rigidify a distorted view of the world. Neurotic pride, for instance, fosters egocentricity, encourages experiencing others in terms of externalizations, and causes the individual to relate on the basis of neurotic claims. These distortions produce increased vulnerability and greater proliferation of unconscious fears. This in turn causes the pride system to reinforce the basic anxiety that initiated the neurotic development in the first place. The vicious circle produced thereby is merely one of many that add momentum to the neurotic process.

Finally, Horney emphasized a holistic approach in which no aspect of the neurotic structure could be fully understood except in relation to all other aspects, to the whole person, and to the world around him. Only if we become reconciled to the complexities of human psychology and resist a simplistic formula to explain it all, can we hope to understand the neurotic struggle for life.

Psychiatric Glossary

AFFECT: To subjectively experience feeling, as contrasted with "emotions" which are the patterns of behavior that express affect.

AGGRESSIVE: See page 211.

AMBIVALENCE: Eugene Bleuler's name for the tendency of some patients to give equal expression to opposing impulses.

ANALITY: The persistence of early anal erotic impulses shown in the adult by abnormal orderliness, stinginess, obstinacy, and revengefulness.

ANXIETY: A condition of heightened, and often disruptive tension, accompanied by a vague feeling of impending harm. It is anticipatory fear and free-floating. Fear, on the other hand, although the same physiological reaction, is a response to an actual danger. Anxiety is often a response to unconscious conflicts.

AUTISM: A mental condition marked by a tendency to turn away from the outside world and to become self-centered.

CLAIM: See page 213.

COMPULSION: An irresistible impulse to perform some act contrary to one's better judgment or will.

CONFABULATION: Replacement of a gap in memory by a falsification which the subject accepts as correct.

CONNOTATION: The associated or secondary meaning of a word or expression in addition to its explicit or primary meaning.

219

DÉJÀ VU: (French: "already seen") An illusion in which a new situation is incorrectly viewed as a repetition of a previous situation.

DELUSION: A false belief which cannot be corrected by reason and is inappropriate to an individual's age, intellectual level, or cultural and historical context.

DENOTATION: A word that names or signifies something specific.

DEREISTIC: Relating to phantasy or imagination. In dereistic thinking the imagination is given free play in disregard of reality.

EXPANSIVE: See page 215.

EXTERNALIZE: See page 212.

FANTASY OR PHANTASY: Imaginative musing without regard to reality.

HALLUCINATION: A sense perception not founded upon objective reality.

ID: Freud's term for the self-preservative tendencies and the instincts as a totality; the true unconscious. It is the reservoir of instinctive impulses and is dominated by the pleasure principle.

IDEAS OF REFERENCE: Through the mechanism of projection an individual egocentrically believes that he is the object of special and ill-disposed attention from those about him.

INSANITY: A social or legal rather than a medical term indicating a condition which renders the affected person unfit to enjoy liberty of action because of the unreliability of his behavior with concomitant danger to himself and others.

INTERN: A medical graduate serving and residing in a hospital preparatory to his being licensed to practice medicine.

LABILITY: Instability; often used as meaning a state of exaggerated or extreme fluctuations.

MAJOR SOLUTION: See page 215.

MORBID DEPENDENCY: See page 217.

NARCISSIST: See page 215.

NEUROSIS: A relatively minor disorder of the psychic constitution; in contrast with the psychosis, it is less incapacitating, and in it the personality remains more or less intact. (For fuller description see Appendix.)

NEUROTIC PRIDE SYSTEM: See page 215.

OBSESSION: An idea which morbidly dominates the mind constantly, suggesting irrational action.

OEDIPUS COMPLEX: Undue attachment of a child to the parent of the opposite sex and corresponding antagonism toward the parent of the same sex.

PARANOID SCHIZOPHRENIA: A subtype of schizophrenia characterized by autistic, unrealistic thinking, with mental content composed chiefly of delusions of persecution and/or of grandeur, ideas of reference, and often hallucinations. Unpredictable behavior, with a fairly constant attitude of hostility and aggression, often occurs. Excessive religiosity or an expansive delusional system of omnipotence, genius, or special ability may be present.

PATHOGENESIS: The development of morbid conditions or disease.

PATHOLOGY: The science or the study of the origin, nature, and course of diseases.

PHANTASY: See fantasy.

PHOBIA: Any persistent abnormal dread or fear.

PSYCHIATRIST: An expert in psychiatry.

PSYCHIATRY: That branch of medicine which deals with mental disorders; the recognition and treatment of mental disorders.

PSYCHIC: Pertaining to the mind; mental.

PSYCHIC CONFLICT: The dilemma in which an individual is impelled by mutually incompatible mental forces and irreconcilable, competing impulses and personality needs.

PSYCHOANALYSIS: The method of eliciting from nervous patients an idea of their past emotional experiences and the facts of their mental life, in order to discover the mechanism by which a pathologic mental state has been produced, and to furnish hints for psychotherapeutic procedures.

PSYCHODYNAMICS: The systematic study of personality in terms of past and present experiences as related to motivation.

PSYCHOLOGY: That branch of science which deals with the mind and mental operations, especially as they are shown in behavior.

PSYCHOMOTOR: Pertaining to motor effects of cerebral or psychic activity.

PSYCHOPATH (OR SOCIOPATH): An individual who is ill, not only in terms of personal discomfort and relations with other individuals, but primarily in terms of society and conforming with the prevailing cultural milieu.

PSYCHOPATHOLOGY: The study of psychologic and behavioral dysfunction in mental disorder.

PSYCHOSIS: Any major, severe form of mental disorder or disease. It is usually characterized by varying degrees of personality disintegration and failure to test and evaluate correctly external reality in various spheres.

RATIONALIZATION: The mental process by which a plausible explanation is concocted for ideas, beliefs, or activities that we wish to have or do; the real motivation being subconscious or at least obscure.

REPRESSION: The thrusting back from consciousness into the unconscious sphere of ideas or perceptions of a disagreeable nature.

RESIDENT: A physician serving full-time on a hospital staff and often living on the premises in order to gain advanced training in a particular field.

RESIGNATION: See page 217.

SCHIZO-AFFECTIVE: Cases showing significant admixtures of schizophrenic and affective reactions. The mental content may be predominantly schizophrenic, with pronounced elation or depression. Cases may show predominantly affective changes with schizophreniclike thinking or bizarre behavior. Most cases prove to be basically schizophrenic on prolonged observation.

SCHIZOID: Resembling schizophrenia; a term supplied by Bleuler to the shut-in, unsocial, introspective type of personality.

SCHIZOPHRENIA: This term is synonymous with the formerly used term *dementia praecox.* It represents a group of psychotic reactions characterized by fundamental disturbances in reality relationships and concept formations, with affective, behavioral, and intellectual disturbances in varying degrees and mixtures. The disorders are marked by strong tendencies to retreat from reality, by emotional disharmony, unpredictable disturbances in the stream of thought, regressive behavior, and in some cases by a tendency toward "deterioration."

SELF-EFFACEMENT: See page 216.

SELF-IDEALIZATION: See page 213.

SELF-REALIZATION: See page 210.

SHOULD: See page 214.

SUGGESTIBILITY: A condition of enfeebled will, with abnormal susceptibility to suggestions.

SUPEREGO: That part of the mental apparatus which acts as a monitor over the ego.